CAMBRIDGE

IELTS

ACADEMIC 14

WITH ANSWERS

AUTHENTIC PRACTICE TESTS

Cambridge University Press
www.cambridge.org/elt

Cambridge Assessment English
www.cambridgeenglish.org

Information on this title: www.cambridge.org/9781108717779

© Cambridge University Press and UCLES 2019

First published 2019

20 19 18 17 16 15 14 13 12 11 10 9 8 7 6 5 4 3 2

Printed in China by CNPIEC Beijing Congreat Printing Co., Ltd

A catalogue record for this publication is available from the British Library

ISBN 978-1-108-69492-6 Academic Student's Book with answers with Audio China reprint edition for
New Oriental School
ISBN 978-1-108-69485-8 Academic Student's Book with answers with Audio China reprint edition
ISBN 978-1-108-71777-9 Academic Student's Book with answers
ISBN 978-1-108-68131-5 Academic Student's Book with answers with Audio
ISBN 978-1-108-69486-5 General Training Student's Book with answers with Audio China reprint edition
ISBN 978-1-108-71779-3 General Training Student's Book with answers
ISBN 978-1-108-68136-0 General Training Student's Book with answers with Audio
ISBN 978-1-108-71860-8 Audio CDs (2)

Contents

Introduction   4

Test 1   10

Test 2   32

Test 3   53

Test 4   75

Audioscripts   97

Listening and Reading answer keys   119

Sample answers for Writing tasks   127

Sample answer sheets   137

Acknowledgements   141

Introduction

The International English Language Testing System (IELTS) is widely recognised as a reliable means of assessing the language ability of candidates who need to study or work where English is the language of communication. These Practice Tests are designed to give future IELTS candidates an idea of whether their English is at the required level.

IELTS is owned by three partners: Cambridge Assessment English, part of the University of Cambridge; the British Council; IDP Education Pty Limited (through its subsidiary company, IELTS Australia Pty Limited). Further information on IELTS can be found on the IELTS website www.ielts.org.

WHAT IS THE TEST FORMAT?

IELTS consists of four components. All candidates take the same Listening and Speaking tests. There is a choice of Reading and Writing tests according to whether a candidate is taking the Academic or General Training module.

Academic	General Training
For candidates wishing to study at undergraduate or postgraduate levels, and for those seeking professional registration.	For candidates wishing to migrate to an English-speaking country (Australia, Canada, New Zealand, UK), and for those wishing to train or study at below degree level.

The test components are taken in the following order:

Listening		
4 sections, 40 items, approximately 30 minutes		
Academic Reading 3 sections, 40 items 60 minutes	or	**General Training Reading** 3 sections, 40 items 60 minutes
Academic Writing 2 tasks 60 minutes	or	**General Training Writing** 2 tasks 60 minutes
Speaking 11 to 14 minutes		
Total Test Time 2 hours 44 minutes		

ACADEMIC TEST FORMAT

Listening

This test consists of four sections, each with ten questions. The first two sections are concerned with social needs. The first section is a conversation between two speakers and the second section is a monologue. The final two sections are concerned with situations related to educational or training contexts. The third section is a conversation between up to four people and the fourth section is a monologue.

A variety of question types is used, including: multiple choice, matching, plan/map/diagram labelling, form completion, note completion, table completion, flow-chart completion, summary completion, sentence completion and short-answer questions.

Candidates hear the recording once only and answer the questions as they listen. Ten minutes are allowed at the end for candidates to transfer their answers to the answer sheet.

Reading

This test consists of three sections with 40 questions. There are three texts, which are taken from journals, books, magazines and newspapers. The texts are on topics of general interest. At least one text contains detailed logical argument.

A variety of question types is used, including: multiple choice, identifying information (True/False/Not Given), identifying the writer's views/claims (Yes/No/Not Given), matching information, matching headings, matching features, matching sentence endings, sentence completion, summary completion, note completion, table completion, flow-chart completion, diagram label completion and short-answer questions.

Writing

This test consists of two tasks. It is suggested that candidates spend about 20 minutes on Task 1, which requires them to write at least 150 words, and 40 minutes on Task 2, which requires them to write at least 250 words. Task 2 contributes twice as much as Task 1 to the Writing score.

Task 1 requires candidates to look at a diagram or some data (in a graph, table or chart) and to present the information in their own words. They are assessed on their ability to organise, present and possibly compare data, and are required to describe the stages of a process, describe an object or event, or explain how something works.

In Task 2, candidates are presented with a point of view, argument or problem. They are assessed on their ability to present a solution to the problem, present and justify an opinion, compare and contrast evidence and opinions, and to evaluate and challenge ideas, evidence or arguments.

Candidates are also assessed on their ability to write in an appropriate style. More information on assessing the Writing test, including Writing assessment criteria (public version), is available on the IELTS website.

Speaking

This test takes between 11 and 14 minutes and is conducted by a trained examiner. There are three parts:

Part 1

The candidate and the examiner introduce themselves. Candidates then answer general questions about themselves, their home/family, their job/studies, their interests and a wide range of similar familiar topic areas. This part lasts between four and five minutes.

Part 2

The candidate is given a task card with prompts and is asked to talk on a particular topic. The candidate has one minute to prepare and they can make some notes if they wish, before speaking for between one and two minutes. The examiner then asks one or two questions on the same topic.

Part 3

The examiner and the candidate engage in a discussion of more abstract issues which are thematically linked to the topic in Part 2. The discussion lasts between four and five minutes.

The Speaking test assesses whether candidates can communicate effectively in English. The assessment takes into account Fluency and Coherence, Lexical Resource, Grammatical Range and Accuracy, and Pronunciation. More information on assessing the Speaking test, including Speaking assessment criteria (public version), is available on the IELTS website.

HOW IS IELTS SCORED?

IELTS results are reported on a nine-band scale. In addition to the score for overall language ability, IELTS provides a score in the form of a profile for each of the four skills (Listening, Reading, Writing and Speaking). These scores are also reported on a nine-band scale. All scores are recorded on the Test Report Form along with details of the candidate's nationality, first language and date of birth. Each Overall Band Score corresponds to a descriptive statement which gives a summary of the English language ability of a candidate classified at that level. The nine bands and their descriptive statements are as follows:

9   *Expert User* – *Has fully operational command of the language: appropriate, accurate and fluent with complete understanding.*

8   *Very Good User* – *Has fully operational command of the language with only occasional unsystematic inaccuracies and inappropriacies. Misunderstandings may occur in unfamiliar situations. Handles complex detailed argumentation well.*

7   *Good User* – *Has operational command of the language, though with occasional inaccuracies, inappropriacies and misunderstandings in some situations. Generally handles complex language well and understands detailed reasoning.*

6   *Competent User* – *Has generally effective command of the language despite some inaccuracies, inappropriacies and misunderstandings. Can use and understand fairly complex language, particularly in familiar situations.*

5   *Modest User* – *Has partial command of the language, coping with overall meaning in most situations, though is likely to make many mistakes. Should be able to handle basic communication in own field.*

4   *Limited User* – *Basic competence is limited to familiar situations. Has frequent problems in understanding and expression. Is not able to use complex language.*

3   *Extremely Limited User* – *Conveys and understands only general meaning in very familiar situations. Frequent breakdowns in communication occur.*

2   *Intermittent User* – *No real communication is possible except for the most basic information using isolated words or short formulae in familiar situations and to meet immediate needs. Has great difficulty understanding spoken and written English.*

1   *Non User* – *Essentially has no ability to use the language beyond possibly a few isolated words.*

0   *Did not attempt the test* – *No assessable information provided.*

MARKING THE PRACTICE TESTS

Listening and Reading

The answer keys are on pages 119–126.
Each question in the Listening and Reading tests is worth one mark.

Questions which require letter / Roman numeral answers

- For questions where the answers are letters or Roman numerals, you should write *only* the number of answers required. For example, if the answer is a single letter or numeral you should write only one answer. If you have written more letters or numerals than are required, the answer must be marked wrong.

Questions which require answers in the form of words or numbers

- Answers may be written in upper or lower case.
- Words in brackets are *optional* – they are correct, but not necessary.
- Alternative answers are separated by a slash (/).
- If you are asked to write an answer using a certain number of words and/or (a) number(s), you will be penalised if you exceed this. For example, if a question specifies an answer using NO MORE THAN THREE WORDS and the correct answer is 'black leather coat', the answer 'coat of black leather' is *incorrect*.
- In questions where you are expected to complete a gap, you should only transfer the necessary missing word(s) onto the answer sheet. For example, to complete 'in the …', where the correct answer is 'morning', the answer 'in the morning' would be *incorrect*.
- All answers require correct spelling (including words in brackets).
- Both US and UK spelling are acceptable and are included in the answer key.
- All standard alternatives for numbers, dates and currencies are acceptable.
- All standard abbreviations are acceptable.
- You will find additional notes about individual answers in the answer key.

Writing

The sample answers are on pages 127–136. It is not possible for you to give yourself a mark for the Writing tasks. We have provided sample answers (written by candidates), showing their score and the examiner's comments. These sample answers will give you an insight into what is required for the Writing test.

HOW SHOULD YOU INTERPRET YOUR SCORES?

At the end of each Listening and Reading answer key you will find a chart which will help you assess whether, on the basis of your Practice Test results, you are ready to take the IELTS test.

In interpreting your score, there are a number of points you should bear in mind. Your performance in the real IELTS test will be reported in two ways: there will be a Band Score from 1 to 9 for each of the components and an Overall Band Score from 1 to 9, which is the average of your scores in the four components. However, institutions considering your application are advised to look at both the Overall Band Score and the Bands for each component in order to determine whether you have the language skills needed for a particular course of study. For example, if your course involves a lot of reading and writing, but no lectures, listening skills might be less important and a score of 5 in Listening might be acceptable if the Overall Band Score was 7. However, for a course which has lots of lectures and spoken instructions, a score of 5 in Listening might be unacceptable even though the Overall Band Score was 7.

Once you have marked your tests, you should have some idea of whether your listening and reading skills are good enough for you to try the IELTS test. If you did well enough in one component, but not in others, you will have to decide for yourself whether you are ready to take the test.

The Practice Tests have been checked to ensure that they are of approximately the same level of difficulty as the real IELTS test. However, we cannot guarantee that your score in the Practice Tests will be reflected in the real IELTS test. The Practice Tests can only give you an idea of your possible future performance and it is ultimately up to you to make decisions based on your score.

Different institutions accept different IELTS scores for different types of courses. We have based our recommendations on the average scores which the majority of institutions accept. The institution to which you are applying may, of course, require a higher or lower score than most other institutions.

Further information

For more information about IELTS or any other Cambridge Assessment English examination, write to:

Cambridge Assessment English
The Triangle Building
Shaftesbury Road
Cambridge
CB2 8EA

https://support.cambridgeenglish.org
http://www.ielts.org

Test 1

SECTION 1   Questions 1–10

Complete the form below.

Write **ONE WORD AND/OR A NUMBER** for each answer.

CRIME REPORT FORM

Type of crime:	theft
Personal information	

Example

Name	Louise ....*Taylor*.........

Nationality	**1** ....
Date of birth	14 December 1977
Occupation	interior designer
Reason for visit	business (to buy antique **2** ....)
Length of stay	two months
Current address	**3** .... Apartments (No 15)

Details of theft

Items stolen	– a wallet containing approximately **4** £ ....
	– a **5** ....
Date of theft	**6** ....

Possible time and place of theft

Location	outside the **7** .... at about 4 pm
Details of suspect	– some boys asked for the **8** .... then ran off
	– one had a T-shirt with a picture of a tiger
	– he was about 12, slim build with **9** .... hair

Crime reference number allocated

        10 ....

SECTION 2   *Questions 11–20*

Induction talk for new apprentices

Questions 11 and 12

Choose TWO letters, A–E.

Which **TWO** pieces of advice for the first week of an apprenticeship does the manager give?

    A   get to know colleagues
    B   learn from any mistakes
    C   ask lots of questions
    D   react positively to feedback
    E   enjoy new challenges

Questions 13 and 14

Choose TWO letters, A–E.

Which **TWO** things does the manager say mentors can help with?

    A   confidence-building
    B   making career plans
    C   completing difficult tasks
    D   making a weekly timetable
    E   reviewing progress

Questions 15–20

What does the manager say about each of the following aspects of the company policy for apprentices?

*Write the correct letter, **A**, **B** or **C**, next to Questions 15–20.*

A	It is encouraged.
B	There are some restrictions.
C	It is against the rules.

Company policy for apprentices

15 Using the internet   ....

16 Flexible working   ....

17 Booking holidays   ....

18 Working overtime   ....

19 Wearing trainers   ....

20 Bringing food to work   ....

SECTION 3   *Questions 21–30*

Questions 21–25

Choose the correct letter, A, B or C.

Cities built by the sea

21 Carla and Rob were surprised to learn that coastal cities

    A   contain nearly half the world's population.
    B   include most of the world's largest cities.
    C   are growing twice as fast as other cities.

22 According to Rob, building coastal cities near to rivers

    A   may bring pollution to the cities.
    B   may reduce the land available for agriculture.
    C   may mean the countryside is spoiled by industry.

23 What mistake was made when building water drainage channels in Miami in the 1950s?

    A   There were not enough of them.
    B   They were made of unsuitable materials.
    C   They did not allow for the effects of climate change.

24 What do Rob and Carla think that the authorities in Miami should do immediately?

    A   take measures to restore ecosystems
    B   pay for a new flood prevention system
    C   stop disposing of waste materials into the ocean

25 What do they agree should be the priority for international action?

    A   greater coordination of activities
    B   more sharing of information
    C   agreement on shared policies

Test 1

Questions 26–30

What decision do the students make about each of the following parts of their presentation?

Choose **FIVE** answers from the box and write the correct letter, **A–G**, next to Questions 26–30.

Decisions

A	use visuals
B	keep it short
C	involve other students
D	check the information is accurate
E	provide a handout
F	focus on one example
G	do online research

Parts of the presentation

26 Historical background ....

27 Geographical factors ....

28 Past mistakes ....

29 Future risks ....

30 International implications ....

SECTION 4   *Questions 31–40*

Complete the notes below.

*Write **ONE WORD ONLY** for each answer.*

Marine renewable energy (ocean energy)

Introduction

More energy required because of growth in population and **31** ....

What's needed:

*   renewable energy sources
*   methods that won't create pollution

Wave energy

Advantage: waves provide a **32** .... source of renewable energy

Electricity can be generated using offshore or onshore systems

Onshore systems may use a reservoir

Problems:

*   waves can move in any **33** ....
*   movement of sand, etc. on the **34** .... of the ocean may be affected

Tidal energy

Tides are more **35** .... than waves

Planned tidal lagoon in Wales:

*   will be created in a **36** .... at Swansea
*   breakwater (dam) containing 16 turbines
*   rising tide forces water through turbines, generating electricity
*   stored water is released through **37** .... , driving the turbines in the reverse direction

Advantages:

*   not dependent on weather
*   no **38** .... is required to make it work
*   likely to create a number of **39** ....

Problem:

*   may harm fish and birds, e.g. by affecting **40** .... and building up silt

Ocean thermal energy conversion

Uses a difference in temperature between the surface and lower levels
Water brought to the surface in a pipe

READING PASSAGE 1

*You should spend about 20 minutes on **Questions 1–13**, which are based on Reading Passage 1 below.*

THE IMPORTANCE OF CHILDREN'S PLAY

Brick by brick, six-year-old Alice is building a magical kingdom. Imagining fairy-tale turrets and fire-breathing dragons, wicked witches and gallant heroes, she's creating an enchanting world. Although she isn't aware of it, this fantasy is helping her take her first steps towards her capacity for creativity and so it will have important repercussions in her adult life.

Minutes later, Alice has abandoned the kingdom in favour of playing schools with her younger brother. When she bosses him around as his 'teacher', she's practising how to regulate her emotions through pretence. Later on, when they tire of this and settle down with a board game, she's learning about the need to follow rules and take turns with a partner.

'Play in all its rich variety is one of the highest achievements of the human species,' says Dr David Whitebread from the Faculty of Education at the University of Cambridge, UK. 'It underpins how we develop as intellectual, problem-solving adults and is crucial to our success as a highly adaptable species.'

Recognising the importance of play is not new: over two millennia ago, the Greek philosopher Plato extolled its virtues as a means of developing skills for adult life, and ideas about play-based learning have been developing since the 19th century.

But we live in changing times, and Whitebread is mindful of a worldwide decline in play, pointing out that over half the people in the world now live in cities. 'The opportunities for free play, which I experienced almost every day of my childhood, are becoming increasingly scarce,' he says. Outdoor play is curtailed by perceptions of risk to do with traffic, as well as parents' increased wish to protect their children from being the victims of crime, and by the emphasis on 'earlier is better' which is leading to greater competition in academic learning and schools.

International bodies like the United Nations and the European Union have begun to develop policies concerned with children's right to play, and to consider implications for leisure facilities and educational programmes. But what they often lack is the evidence to base policies on.

'The type of play we are interested in is child-initiated, spontaneous and unpredictable – but, as soon as you ask a five-year-old "to play", then you as the researcher have intervened,' explains Dr Sara Baker. 'And we want to know what the long-term impact of play is. It's a real challenge.'

Dr Jenny Gibson agrees, pointing out that although some of the steps in the puzzle of how and why play is important have been looked at, there is very little data on the impact it has on the child's later life.

Now, thanks to the university's new Centre for Research on Play in Education, Development and Learning (PEDAL), Whitebread, Baker, Gibson and a team of researchers hope to provide evidence on the role played by play in how a child develops.

'A strong possibility is that play supports the early development of children's self-control,' explains Baker. 'This is our ability to develop awareness of our own thinking processes – it influences how effectively we go about undertaking challenging activities.'

In a study carried out by Baker with toddlers and young pre-schoolers, she found that children with greater self-control solved problems more quickly when exploring an unfamiliar set-up requiring scientific reasoning. 'This sort of evidence makes us think that giving children the chance to play will make them more successful problem-solvers in the long run.'

If playful experiences do facilitate this aspect of development, say the researchers, it could be extremely significant for educational practices, because the ability to self-regulate has been shown to be a key predictor of academic performance.

Gibson adds: 'Playful behaviour is also an important indicator of healthy social and emotional development. In my previous research, I investigated how observing children at play can give us important clues about their well-being and can even be useful in the diagnosis of neurodevelopmental disorders like autism.'

Whitebread's recent research has involved developing a play-based approach to supporting children's writing. 'Many primary school children find writing difficult, but we showed in a previous study that a playful stimulus was far more effective than an instructional one.' Children wrote longer and better-structured stories when they first played with dolls representing characters in the story. In the latest study, children first created their story with Lego*, with similar results. 'Many teachers commented that they had always previously had children saying they didn't know what to write about. With the Lego building, however, not a single child said this through the whole year of the project.'

Whitebread, who directs PEDAL, trained as a primary school teacher in the early 1970s, when, as he describes, 'the teaching of young children was largely a quiet backwater, untroubled by any serious intellectual debate or controversy.' Now, the landscape is very different, with hotly debated topics such as school starting age.

'Somehow the importance of play has been lost in recent decades. It's regarded as something trivial, or even as something negative that contrasts with "work". Let's not lose sight of its benefits, and the fundamental contributions it makes to human achievements in the arts, sciences and technology. Let's make sure children have a rich diet of play experiences.'

---

* Lego: coloured plastic building blocks and other pieces that can be joined together

Test 1

Questions 1–8

Complete the notes below.

*Choose **ONE WORD ONLY** from the passage for each answer.*

Write your answers in boxes 1–8 on your answer sheet.

Children's play

Uses of children's play

- building a 'magical kingdom' may help develop **1** ....
- board games involve **2** .... and turn-taking

Recent changes affecting children's play

- populations of **3** .... have grown
- opportunities for free play are limited due to
  - fear of **4** ....
  - fear of **5** ....
  - increased **6** .... in schools

International policies on children's play

- it is difficult to find **7** .... to support new policies
- research needs to study the impact of play on the rest of the child's **8** ....

Questions 9–13

Do the following statements agree with the information given in Reading Passage 1?

In boxes 9–13 on your answer sheet, write

> **TRUE**   *if the statement agrees with the information*
> **FALSE**   *if the statement contradicts the information*
> **NOT GIVEN** *if there is no information on this*

9   Children with good self-control are known to be likely to do well at school later on.

10 The way a child plays may provide information about possible medical problems.

11 Playing with dolls was found to benefit girls' writing more than boys' writing.

12 Children had problems thinking up ideas when they first created the story with Lego.

13 People nowadays regard children's play as less significant than they did in the past.

READING PASSAGE 2

*You should spend about 20 minutes on **Questions 14–26**, which are based on Reading Passage 2 below.*

The growth of bike-sharing schemes around the world

How Dutch engineer Luud Schimmelpennink helped to devise urban bike-sharing schemes

A   The original idea for an urban bike-sharing scheme dates back to a summer's day in Amsterdam in 1965. Provo, the organisation that came up with the idea, was a group of Dutch activists who wanted to change society. They believed the scheme, which was known as the Witte Fietsenplan, was an answer to the perceived threats of air pollution and consumerism. In the centre of Amsterdam, they painted a small number of used bikes white. They also distributed leaflets describing the dangers of cars and inviting people to use the white bikes. The bikes were then left unlocked at various locations around the city, to be used by anyone in need of transport.

B   Luud Schimmelpennink, a Dutch industrial engineer who still lives and cycles in Amsterdam, was heavily involved in the original scheme. He recalls how the scheme succeeded in attracting a great deal of attention – particularly when it came to publicising Provo's aims – but struggled to get off the ground. The police were opposed to Provo's initiatives and almost as soon as the white bikes were distributed around the city, they removed them. However, for Schimmelpennink and for bike-sharing schemes in general, this was just the beginning. 'The first Witte Fietsenplan was just a symbolic thing,' he says. 'We painted a few bikes white, that was all. Things got more serious when I became a member of the Amsterdam city council two years later.'

C   Schimmelpennink seized this opportunity to present a more elaborate Witte Fietsenplan to the city council. 'My idea was that the municipality of Amsterdam would distribute 10,000 white bikes over the city, for everyone to use,' he explains. 'I made serious calculations. It turned out that a white bicycle – per person, per kilometre – would cost the municipality only 10% of what it contributed to public transport per person per kilometre.' Nevertheless, the council unanimously rejected the plan. 'They said that the bicycle belongs to the past. They saw a glorious future for the car,' says Schimmelpennink. But he was not in the least discouraged.

D   Schimmelpennink never stopped believing in bike-sharing, and in the mid-90s, two Danes asked for his help to set up a system in Copenhagen. The result was the world's first large-scale bike-share programme. It worked on a deposit: 'You dropped a coin in the bike and when you returned it, you got your money back.' After setting up the Danish system, Schimmelpennink decided to try his luck again in the Netherlands – and this time he succeeded in arousing the interest of the Dutch Ministry of Transport. 'Times had changed,' he recalls. 'People had become more environmentally conscious, and the Danish experiment had proved that bike-sharing was a real possibility.' A new Witte Fietsenplan was launched in 1999 in Amsterdam. However, riding a white bike was no longer free; it cost one guilder per trip and payment was made with a chip card developed by the Dutch bank Postbank. Schimmelpennink designed conspicuous, sturdy white bikes locked in special racks which could be opened with the chip card – the plan started with 250 bikes, distributed over five stations.

E   Theo Molenaar, who was a system designer for the project, worked alongside Schimmelpennink. 'I remember when we were testing the bike racks, he announced that he had already designed better ones. But of course, we had to go through with the ones we had.' The system, however, was prone to vandalism and theft. 'After every weekend there would always be a couple of bikes missing,' Molenaar says. 'I really have no idea what people did with them, because they could instantly be recognised as white bikes.' But the biggest blow came when Postbank decided to abolish the chip card, because it wasn't profitable. 'That chip card was pivotal to the system,' Molenaar says. 'To continue the project we would have needed to set up another system, but the business partner had lost interest.'

F   Schimmelpennink was disappointed, but – characteristically – not for long. In 2002 he got a call from the French advertising corporation JC Decaux, who wanted to set up his bike-sharing scheme in Vienna. 'That went really well. After Vienna, they set up a system in Lyon. Then in 2007, Paris followed. That was a decisive moment in the history of bike-sharing.' The huge and unexpected success of the Parisian bike-sharing programme, which now boasts more than 20,000 bicycles, inspired cities all over the world to set up their own schemes, all modelled on Schimmelpennink's. 'It's wonderful that this happened,' he says. 'But financially I didn't really benefit from it, because I never filed for a patent.'

G   In Amsterdam today, 38% of all trips are made by bike and, along with Copenhagen, it is regarded as one of the two most cycle-friendly capitals in the world – but the city never got another Witte Fietsenplan. Molenaar believes this may be because everybody in Amsterdam already has a bike. Schimmelpennink, however, cannot see that this changes Amsterdam's need for a bike-sharing scheme. 'People who travel on the underground don't carry their bikes around. But often they need additional transport to reach their final destination.' Although he thinks it is strange that a city like Amsterdam does not have a successful bike-sharing scheme, he is optimistic about the future. 'In the '60s we didn't stand a chance because people were prepared to give their lives to keep cars in the city. But that mentality has totally changed. Today everybody longs for cities that are not dominated by cars.'

Questions 14–18

Reading Passage 2 has seven paragraphs, **A–G**.

Which paragraph contains the following information?

*Write the correct letter, **A–G**, in boxes 14–18 on your answer sheet.*

NB   You may use any letter more than once.

14   a description of how people misused a bike-sharing scheme

15   an explanation of why a proposed bike-sharing scheme was turned down

16   a reference to a person being unable to profit from their work

17   an explanation of the potential savings a bike-sharing scheme would bring

18   a reference to the problems a bike-sharing scheme was intended to solve

Questions 19 and 20

*Choose **TWO** letters, **A–E**.*

Write the correct letters in boxes 19 and 20 on your answer sheet.

Which **TWO** of the following statements are made in the text about the Amsterdam bike-sharing scheme of 1999?

A   It was initially opposed by a government department.
B   It failed when a partner in the scheme withdrew support.
C   It aimed to be more successful than the Copenhagen scheme.
D   It was made possible by a change in people's attitudes.
E   It attracted interest from a range of bike designers.

Questions 21 and 22

Choose *TWO* letters, *A–E*.

Write the correct letters in boxes 21 and 22 on your answer sheet.

Which **TWO** of the following statements are made in the text about Amsterdam today?

<table>
<tr><td>A</td><td>The majority of residents would like to prevent all cars from entering the city.</td></tr>
<tr><td>B</td><td>There is little likelihood of the city having another bike-sharing scheme.</td></tr>
<tr><td>C</td><td>More trips in the city are made by bike than by any other form of transport.</td></tr>
<tr><td>D</td><td>A bike-sharing scheme would benefit residents who use public transport.</td></tr>
<tr><td>E</td><td>The city has a reputation as a place that welcomes cyclists.</td></tr>
</table>

Questions 23–26

Complete the summary below.

Choose **ONE WORD ONLY** from the passage for each answer.

Write your answers in boxes 23–26 on your answer sheet.

The first urban bike-sharing scheme

The first bike-sharing scheme was the idea of the Dutch group Provo. The people who belonged to this group were **23** .... They were concerned about damage to the environment and about **24** .... , and believed that the bike-sharing scheme would draw attention to these issues. As well as painting some bikes white, they handed out **25** .... that condemned the use of cars.

However, the scheme was not a great success: almost as quickly as Provo left the bikes around the city, the **26** .... took them away. According to Schimmelpennink, the scheme was intended to be symbolic. The idea was to get people thinking about the issues.

READING PASSAGE 3

*You should spend about 20 minutes on **Questions 27–40**, which are based on Reading Passage 3 below.*

Motivational factors and the hospitality industry

A critical ingredient in the success of hotels is developing and maintaining superior performance from their employees. How is that accomplished? What Human Resource Management (HRM) practices should organizations invest in to acquire and retain great employees?

Some hotels aim to provide superior working conditions for their employees. The idea originated from workplaces – usually in the non-service sector – that emphasized fun and enjoyment as part of work–life balance. By contrast, the service sector, and more specifically hotels, has traditionally not extended these practices to address basic employee needs, such as good working conditions.

Pfeffer (1994) emphasizes that in order to succeed in a global business environment, organizations must make investment in Human Resource Management (HRM) to allow them to acquire employees who possess better skills and capabilities than their competitors. This investment will be to their competitive advantage. Despite this recognition of the importance of employee development, the hospitality industry has historically been dominated by underdeveloped HR practices (Lucas, 2002).

Lucas also points out that 'the substance of HRM practices does not appear to be designed to foster constructive relations with employees or to represent a managerial approach that enables developing and drawing out the full potential of people, even though employees may be broadly satisfied with many aspects of their work' (Lucas, 2002). In addition, or maybe as a result, high employee turnover has been a recurring problem throughout the hospitality industry. Among the many cited reasons are low compensation, inadequate benefits, poor working conditions and compromised employee morale and attitudes (Maroudas et al., 2008).

Ng and Sorensen (2008) demonstrated that when managers provide recognition to employees, motivate employees to work together, and remove obstacles preventing effective performance, employees feel more obligated to stay with the company. This was succinctly summarized by Michel et al. (2013): '[P]roviding support to employees gives them the confidence to perform their jobs better and the motivation to stay with the organization.' Hospitality organizations can therefore enhance employee motivation and retention through the development and improvement of their working conditions. These conditions are inherently linked to the working environment.

While it seems likely that employees' reactions to their job characteristics could be affected by a predisposition to view their work environment negatively, no evidence exists to support this hypothesis (Spector et al., 2000). However, given the opportunity, many people will find something to complain about in relation to their workplace (Poulston, 2009). There is a strong link between the perceptions of employees and particular factors of their work environment that are separate from the work itself, including company policies, salary and vacations.

Such conditions are particularly troubling for the luxury hotel market, where high-quality service, requiring a sophisticated approach to HRM, is recognized as a critical source of competitive advantage (Maroudas et al., 2008). In a real sense, the services of hotel employees represent their industry (Schneider and Bowen, 1993). This representation has commonly been limited to guest experiences. This suggests that there has been a dichotomy between the guest environment provided in luxury hotels and the working conditions of their employees.

It is therefore essential for hotel management to develop HRM practices that enable them to inspire and retain competent employees. This requires an understanding of what motivates employees at different levels of management and different stages of their careers (Enz and Siguaw, 2000). This implies that it is beneficial for hotel managers to understand what practices are most favorable to increase employee satisfaction and retention.

Herzberg (1966) proposes that people have two major types of needs, the first being extrinsic motivation factors relating to the context in which work is performed, rather than the work itself. These include working conditions and job security. When these factors are unfavorable, job dissatisfaction may result. Significantly, though, just fulfilling these needs does not result in satisfaction, but only in the reduction of dissatisfaction (Maroudas et al., 2008).

Employees also have intrinsic motivation needs or motivators, which include such factors as achievement and recognition. Unlike extrinsic factors, motivator factors may ideally result in job satisfaction (Maroudas et al., 2008). Herzberg's (1966) theory discusses the need for a 'balance' of these two types of needs.

The impact of fun as a motivating factor at work has also been explored. For example, Tews, Michel and Stafford (2013) conducted a study focusing on staff from a chain of themed restaurants in the United States. It was found that fun activities had a favorable impact on performance and manager support for fun had a favorable impact in reducing turnover. Their findings support the view that fun may indeed have a beneficial effect, but the framing of that fun must be carefully aligned with both organizational goals and employee characteristics. 'Managers must learn how to achieve the delicate balance of allowing employees the freedom to enjoy themselves at work while simultaneously maintaining high levels of performance' (Tews et al., 2013).

Deery (2008) has recommended several actions that can be adopted at the organizational level to retain good staff as well as assist in balancing work and family life. Those particularly appropriate to the hospitality industry include allowing adequate breaks during the working day, staff functions that involve families, and providing health and well-being opportunities.

Questions 27–31

Look at the following statements (Questions 27–31) and the list of researchers below.

*Match each statement with the correct researcher, **A–F**.*

*Write the correct letter, **A–F**, in boxes 27–31 on your answer sheet.*

NB *You may use any letter more than once.*

27   Hotel managers need to know what would encourage good staff to remain.

28   The actions of managers may make staff feel they shouldn't move to a different employer.

29   Little is done in the hospitality industry to help workers improve their skills.

30   Staff are less likely to change jobs if cooperation is encouraged.

31   Dissatisfaction with pay is not the only reason why hospitality workers change jobs.

List of Researchers

A   Pfeffer

B   Lucas

C   Maroudas et al.

D   Ng and Sorensen

E   Enz and Siguaw

F   Deery

Questions 32–35

Do the following statements agree with the claims of the writer in Reading **Passage 3**?

In boxes 32–35 on your answer sheet, write

> **YES**   *if the statement agrees with the claims of the writer*
> **NO**   *if the statement contradicts the claims of the writer*
> **NOT GIVEN** *if it is impossible to say what the writer thinks about this*

32   One reason for high staff turnover in the hospitality industry is poor morale.

33   Research has shown that staff have a tendency to dislike their workplace.

34   An improvement in working conditions and job security makes staff satisfied with their jobs.

35   Staff should be allowed to choose when they take breaks during the working day.

Questions 36–40

Complete the summary below.

*Choose **ONE WORD ONLY** from the passage for each answer.*

Write your answers in boxes 36–40 on your answer sheet.

Fun at work

Tews, Michel and Stafford carried out research on staff in an American chain of
36 .... They discovered that activities designed for staff to have fun
improved their 37 .... , and that management involvement led to lower
staff 38 .... They also found that the activities needed to fit with both the
company's 39 .... and the 40 .... of the staff. A balance was
required between a degree of freedom and maintaining work standards.

WRITING

WRITING TASK 1

You should spend about 20 minutes on this task.

> *The charts below show the average percentages in typical meals of three types of nutrients, all of which may be unhealthy if eaten too much.*
>
> *Summarise the information by selecting and reporting the main features, and make comparisons where relevant.*

Write at least 150 words.

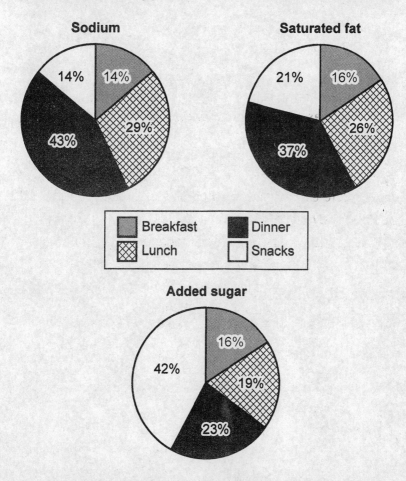

Average percentages of sodium, saturated fats and added sugars in typical meals consumed in the USA

WRITING TASK 2

You should spend about 40 minutes on this task.

Write about the following topic:

> *Some people believe that it is best to accept a bad situation, such as an unsatisfactory job or shortage of money. Others argue that it is better to try and improve such situations.*
>
> *Discuss both these views and give your own opinion.*

Give reasons for your answer and include any relevant examples from your own knowledge or experience.

Write at least 250 words.

SPEAKING

PART 1

The examiner asks the candidate about him/herself, his/her home, work or studies and other familiar topics.

EXAMPLE

Future

- What job would you like to have ten years from now? [Why?]
- How useful will English be for your future? [Why/Why not?]
- How much travelling do you hope to do in the future? [Why/Why not?]
- How do you think your life will change in the future? [Why/Why not?]

PART 2

Describe a book that you enjoyed reading because you had to think a lot.

You should say:
   what this book was
   why you decided to read it
   what reading this book made you think about

and explain why you enjoyed reading this book.

You will have to talk about the topic for one to two minutes. You have one minute to think about what you are going to say. You can make some notes to help you if you wish.

PART 3

Discussion topics:

Children and reading

Example questions:
What are the most popular types of children's books in your country?
What are the benefits of parents reading books to their children?
Should parents always let children choose the books they read?

Electronic books

Example questions:
How popular are electronic books are in your country?
What are the advantages of parents reading electronic books (compared to printed books)?
Will electronic books ever completely replace printed books in the future?

Test 2

SECTION 1   Questions 1–10

Complete the notes below.

Write **ONE WORD AND/OR A NUMBER** for each answer.

TOTAL HEALTH CLINIC

PATIENT DETAILS

Personal information

Example

Name   Julie Anne ....*Garcia*........

Contact phone	**1** ....
Date of birth	**2** .... , 1992
Occupation	works as a **3** ....
Insurance company	**4** .... Life Insurance

Details of the problem

Type of problem	pain in her left **5** ....
When it began	**6** .... ago
Action already taken	has taken painkillers and applied ice

Other information

Sports played	belongs to a **7** .... club
	goes **8** .... regularly
Medical history	injured her **9** .... last year
	no allergies
	no regular medication apart from **10** ....

SECTION 2   *Questions 11–20*

Questions 11–15

Choose the correct letter, A, B or C.

Visit to Branley Castle

11   Before Queen Elizabeth I visited the castle in 1576,

A   repairs were carried out to the guest rooms.
B   a new building was constructed for her.
C   a fire damaged part of the main hall.

12   In 1982, the castle was sold to

A   the government.
B   the Fenys family.
C   an entertainment company.

13   In some of the rooms, visitors can

A   speak to experts on the history of the castle.
B   interact with actors dressed as famous characters.
C   see models of historical figures moving and talking.

14   In the castle park, visitors can

A   see an 800-year-old tree.
B   go to an art exhibition.
C   visit a small zoo.

15   At the end of the visit, the group will have

A   afternoon tea in the conservatory.
B   the chance to meet the castle's owners.
C   a photograph together on the Great Staircase.

Questions 16–20

Label the plan below.

Write the correct letter, **A–H**, next to Questions 16–20.

Branley Castle

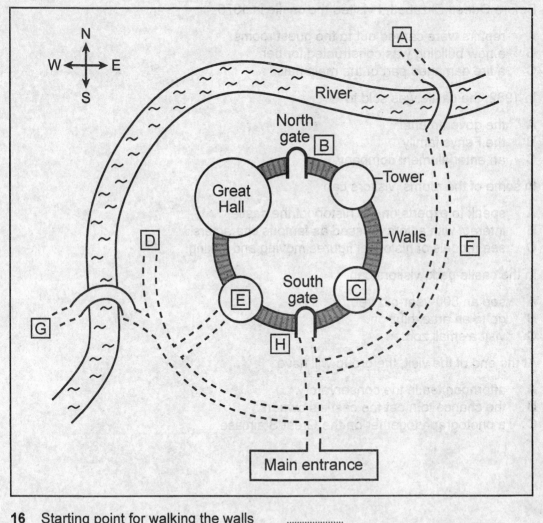

16 Starting point for walking the walls   ....

17 Bow and arrow display   ....

18 Hunting birds display   ....

19 Traditional dancing   ....

20 Shop   ....

SECTION 3   *Questions 21–30*

Questions 21–24

Choose the correct letter, A, B or C.

Woolly mammoths on St Paul's Island

21 How will Rosie and Martin introduce their presentation?

    A   with a drawing of woolly mammoths in their natural habitat
    B   with a timeline showing when woolly mammoths lived
    C   with a video clip about woolly mammoths

22 What was surprising about the mammoth tooth found by Russell Graham?

    A   It was still embedded in the mammoth's jawbone.
    B   It was from an unknown species of mammoth.
    C   It was not as old as mammoth remains from elsewhere.

23 The students will use an animated diagram to demonstrate how the mammoths

    A   became isolated on the island.
    B   spread from the island to other areas.
    C   coexisted with other animals on the island.

24 According to Martin, what is unusual about the date of the mammoths' extinction on the island?

    A   how exact it is
    B   how early it is
    C   how it was established

Questions 25–30

What action will the students take for each of the following sections of their presentation?

Choose SIX answers from the box and write the correct letter, A–H, next to Questions 25–30.

```
                    Actions
    A    make it more interactive
    B    reduce visual input
    C    add personal opinions
    D    contact one of the researchers
    E    make detailed notes
    F    find information online
    G    check timing
    H    organise the content more clearly
```

Sections of presentation

25 Introduction   ....

26 Discovery of the mammoth tooth   ....

27 Initial questions asked by the researchers   ....

28 Further research carried out on the island   ....

29 Findings and possible explanations   ....

30 Relevance to the present day   ....

SECTION 4   *Questions 31–40*

Complete the notes below.

*Write **ONE WORD ONLY** for each answer.*

The history of weather forecasting

Ancient cultures

- many cultures believed that floods and other disasters were involved in the creation of the world

- many cultures invented **31** .... and other ceremonies to make the weather gods friendly

- people needed to observe and interpret the sky to ensure their **32** ....

- around 650 BC, Babylonians started forecasting, using weather phenomena such as **33** ....

- by 300 BC, the Chinese had a calendar made up of a number of **34** .... connected with the weather

Ancient Greeks

- a more scientific approach

- Aristotle tried to explain the formation of various weather phenomena

- Aristotle also described haloes and **35** ....

Middle Ages

- Aristotle's work considered accurate

- many proverbs, e.g. about the significance of the colour of the **36** ...., passed on accurate information.

15th–19th centuries

- 15th century: scientists recognised value of **37** .... for the first time

- Galileo invented the **38** ....

- Pascal showed relationship between atmospheric pressure and altitude

- from the 17th century, scientists could measure atmospheric pressure and temperature

- 18th century: Franklin identified the movement of **39** ....

- 19th century: data from different locations could be sent to the same place by **40** ....

READING

READING PASSAGE 1

*You should spend about 20 minutes on **Questions 1–13**, which are based on Reading Passage 1 below.*

Alexander Henderson (1831–1913)

Born in Scotland, Henderson emigrated to Canada in 1855 and became a well-known landscape photographer

Alexander Henderson was born in Scotland in 1831 and was the son of a successful merchant. His grandfather, also called Alexander, had founded the family business, and later became the first chairman of the National Bank of Scotland. The family had extensive landholdings in Scotland. Besides its residence in Edinburgh, it owned Press Estate, 650 acres of farmland about 35 miles southeast of the city. The family often stayed at Press Castle, the large mansion on the northern edge of the property, and Alexander spent much of his childhood in the area, playing on the beach near Eyemouth or fishing in the streams nearby.

Even after he went to school at Murcheston Academy on the outskirts of Edinburgh, Henderson returned to Press at weekends. In 1849 he began a three-year apprenticeship to become an accountant. Although he never liked the prospect of a business career, he stayed with it to please his family. In October 1855, however, he emigrated to Canada with his wife Agnes Elder Robertson and they settled in Montreal.

Henderson learned photography in Montreal around the year 1857 and quickly took it up as a serious amateur. He became a personal friend and colleague of the Scottish–Canadian photographer William Notman. The two men made a photographic excursion to Niagara Falls in 1860 and they cooperated on experiments with magnesium flares as a source of artificial light in 1865. They belonged to the same societies and were among the founding members of the Art Association of Montreal. Henderson acted as chairman of the association's first meeting, which was held in Notman's studio on 11 January 1860.

In spite of their friendship, their styles of photography were quite different. While Notman's landscapes were noted for their bold realism, Henderson for the first 20 years of his career produced romantic images, showing the strong influence of the British landscape tradition. His artistic and technical progress was rapid and in 1865 he published his first major collection of landscape photographs. The publication had limited circulation (only seven copies have ever been found), and was called *Canadian Views and Studies*. The contents of each copy vary significantly and have proved a useful source for evaluating Henderson's early work.

This text is taken, for the most part, verbatim from the *Dictionary of Canadian Biography* Volume XIV (1911–1920). For design purposes, quotation marks have been omitted. Source: http://www.biographi.ca/en/bio/henderson_alexander_1831_1913_14E.html. Reproduced with permission.

In 1866, he gave up his business to open a photographic studio, advertising himself as a portrait and landscape photographer. From about 1870 he dropped portraiture to specialize in landscape photography and other views. His numerous photographs of city life revealed in street scenes, houses, and markets are alive with human activity, and although his favourite subject was landscape he usually composed his scenes around such human pursuits as farming the land, cutting ice on a river, or sailing down a woodland stream. There was sufficient demand for these types of scenes and others he took depicting the lumber trade, steamboats and waterfalls to enable him to make a living. There was little competing hobby or amateur photography before the late 1880s because of the time-consuming techniques involved and the weight of the equipment. People wanted to buy photographs as souvenirs of a trip or as gifts, and catering to this market, Henderson had stock photographs on display at his studio for mounting, framing, or inclusion in albums.

Henderson frequently exhibited his photographs in Montreal and abroad, in London, Edinburgh, Dublin, Paris, New York, and Philadelphia. He met with greater success in 1877 and 1878 in New York when he won first prizes in the exhibition held by E and H T Anthony and Company for landscapes using the Lambertype process. In 1878 his work won second prize at the world exhibition in Paris.

In the 1870s and 1880s Henderson travelled widely throughout Quebec and Ontario, in Canada, documenting the major cities of the two provinces and many of the villages in Quebec. He was especially fond of the wilderness and often travelled by canoe on the Blanche, du Lièvre, and other noted eastern rivers. He went on several occasions to the Maritimes and in 1872 he sailed by yacht along the lower north shore of the St Lawrence River. That same year, while in the lower St Lawrence River region, he took some photographs of the construction of the Intercolonial Railway. This undertaking led in 1875 to a commission from the railway to record the principal structures along the almost-completed line connecting Montreal to Halifax. Commissions from other railways followed. In 1876 he photographed bridges on the Quebec, Montreal, Ottawa and Occidental Railway between Montreal and Ottawa. In 1885 he went west along the Canadian Pacific Railway (CPR) as far as Rogers Pass in British Columbia, where he took photographs of the mountains and the progress of construction.

In 1892 Henderson accepted a full-time position with the CPR as manager of a photographic department which he was to set up and administer. His duties included spending four months in the field each year. That summer he made his second trip west, photographing extensively along the railway line as far as Victoria. He continued in this post until 1897, when he retired completely from photography.

When Henderson died in 1913, his huge collection of glass negatives was stored in the basement of his house. Today collections of his work are held at the National Archives of Canada, Ottawa, and the McCord Museum of Canadian History, Montreal.

This text is taken, for the most part, verbatim from the *Dictionary of Canadian Biography* Volume XIV (1911–1920). For design purposes, quotation marks have been omitted. Source: http://www.biographi.ca/en/bio/henderson_alexander_1831_1913_14E.html. Reproduced with permission.

Questions 1–8

Do the following statements agree with the information given in Reading Passage 1?

In boxes 1–8 on your answer sheet, write

> **TRUE**   *if the statement agrees with the information*
> **FALSE**   *if the statement contradicts the information*
> **NOT GIVEN**   *if there is no information on this*

1   Henderson rarely visited the area around Press estate when he was younger.

2   Henderson pursued a business career because it was what his family wanted.

3   Henderson and Notman were surprised by the results of their 1865 experiment.

4   There were many similarities between Henderson's early landscapes and those of Notman.

5   The studio that Henderson opened in 1866 was close to his home.

6   Henderson gave up portraiture so that he could focus on taking photographs of scenery.

7   When Henderson began work for the Intercolonial Railway, the Montreal to Halifax line had been finished.

8   Henderson's last work as a photographer was with the Canadian Pacific Railway.

Questions 9–13

Complete the notes below.

*Choose **ONE WORD ONLY** from the passage for each answer.*

Write your answers in boxes 9–13 on your answer sheet.

Alexander Henderson

Early life

- was born in Scotland in 1831 – father was a **9** ....

- trained as an accountant, emigrated to Canada in 1855

Start of a photographic career

- opened up a photographic studio in 1866

- took photos of city life, but preferred landscape photography

- people bought Henderson's photos because photography took up considerable time and the **10** .... was heavy

- the photographs Henderson sold were **11** .... or souvenirs

Travelling as a professional photographer

- travelled widely in Quebec and Ontario in 1870s and 1880s

- took many trips along eastern rivers in a **12** ....

- worked for Canadian railways between 1875 and 1897

- worked for CPR in 1885 and photographed the **13** .... and the railway at Rogers Pass

---

READING PASSAGE 2

You should spend about 20 minutes on **Questions 14–26,** which are based on Reading Passage 2 below.

Back to the future of skyscraper design

Answers to the problem of excessive electricity use by skyscrapers and large public buildings can be found in ingenious but forgotten architectural designs of the 19th and early-20th centuries

A   *The Recovery of Natural Environments in Architecture* by Professor Alan Short is the culmination of 30 years of research and award-winning green building design by Short and colleagues in Architecture, Engineering, Applied Maths and Earth Sciences at the University of Cambridge.

'The crisis in building design is already here,' said Short. 'Policy makers think you can solve energy and building problems with gadgets. You can't. As global temperatures continue to rise, we are going to continue to squander more and more energy on keeping our buildings mechanically cool until we have run out of capacity.'

B   Short is calling for a sweeping reinvention of how skyscrapers and major public buildings are designed – to end the reliance on sealed buildings which exist solely via the 'life support' system of vast air conditioning units.

Instead, he shows it is entirely possible to accommodate natural ventilation and cooling in large buildings by looking into the past, before the widespread introduction of air conditioning systems, which were 'relentlessly and aggressively marketed' by their inventors.

C   Short points out that to make most contemporary buildings habitable, they have to be sealed and air conditioned. The energy use and carbon emissions this generates is spectacular and largely unnecessary. Buildings in the West account for 40–50% of electricity usage, generating substantial carbon emissions, and the rest of the world is catching up at a frightening rate. Short regards glass, steel and air-conditioned skyscrapers as symbols of status, rather than practical ways of meeting our requirements.

D   Short's book highlights a developing and sophisticated art and science of ventilating buildings through the 19th and earlier-20th centuries, including the design of ingeniously ventilated hospitals. Of particular interest were those built to the designs of John Shaw Billings, including the first Johns Hopkins Hospital in the US city of Baltimore (1873–1889).

'We spent three years digitally modelling Billings' final designs,' says Short. 'We put pathogens* in the airstreams, modelled for someone with tuberculosis (TB) coughing in the wards and we found the ventilation systems in the room would have kept other patients safe from harm.

---

* pathogens: microorganisms that can cause disease

E 'We discovered that 19th-century hospital wards could generate up to 24 air changes an hour – that's similar to the performance of a modern-day, computer-controlled operating theatre. We believe you could build wards based on these principles now.

Single rooms are not appropriate for all patients. Communal wards appropriate for certain patients – older people with dementia, for example – would work just as well in today's hospitals, at a fraction of the energy cost.'

Professor Short contends the mindset and skill-sets behind these designs have been completely lost, lamenting the disappearance of expertly designed theatres, opera houses, and other buildings where up to half the volume of the building was given over to ensuring everyone got fresh air.

F Much of the ingenuity present in 19th-century hospital and building design was driven by a panicked public clamouring for buildings that could protect against what was thought to be the lethal threat of miasmas – toxic air that spread disease. Miasmas were feared as the principal agents of disease and epidemics for centuries, and were used to explain the spread of infection from the Middle Ages right through to the cholera outbreaks in London and Paris during the 1850s. Foul air, rather than germs, was believed to be the main driver of 'hospital fever', leading to disease and frequent death. The prosperous steered clear of hospitals.

While miasma theory has been long since disproved, Short has for the last 30 years advocated a return to some of the building design principles produced in its wake.

G Today, huge amounts of a building's space and construction cost are given over to air conditioning. 'But I have designed and built a series of buildings over the past three decades which have tried to reinvent some of these ideas and then measure what happens.

'To go forward into our new low-energy, low-carbon future, we would be well advised to look back at design before our high-energy, high-carbon present appeared. What is surprising is what a rich legacy we have abandoned.'

H Successful examples of Short's approach include the Queen's Building at De Montfort University in Leicester. Containing as many as 2,000 staff and students, the entire building is naturally ventilated, passively cooled and naturally lit, including the two largest auditoria, each seating more than 150 people. The award-winning building uses a fraction of the electricity of comparable buildings in the UK.

Short contends that glass skyscrapers in London and around the world will become a liability over the next 20 or 30 years if climate modelling predictions and energy price rises come to pass as expected.

I He is convinced that sufficiently cooled skyscrapers using the natural environment can be produced in almost any climate. He and his team have worked on hybrid buildings in the harsh climates of Beijing and Chicago – built with natural ventilation assisted by back-up air conditioning – which, surprisingly perhaps, can be switched off more than half the time on milder days and during the spring and autumn.

Short looks at how we might reimagine the cities, offices and homes of the future. Maybe it's time we changed our outlook.

Questions 14–18

Reading Passage 2 has nine sections, **A–I**.

Which section contains the following information?

Write the correct letter, A–I, in boxes 14–18 on your answer sheet.

14 why some people avoided hospitals in the 19th century

15 a suggestion that the popularity of tall buildings is linked to prestige

16 a comparison between the circulation of air in a 19th-century building and modern standards

17 how Short tested the circulation of air in a 19th-century building

18 an implication that advertising led to the large increase in the use of air conditioning

Questions 19–26

Complete the summary below.

*Choose **ONE WORD ONLY** from the passage for each answer.*

Write your answers in boxes 19–26 on your answer sheet.

Ventilation in 19th-century hospital wards

Professor Alan Short examined the work of John Shaw Billings, who influenced the architectural **19** .... of hospitals to ensure they had good ventilation. He calculated that **20** .... in the air coming from patients suffering from **21** .... would not have harmed other patients. He also found that the air in **22** .... in hospitals could change as often as in a modern operating theatre. He suggests that energy use could be reduced by locating more patients in **23** .... areas.

A major reason for improving ventilation in 19th-century hospitals was the demand from the **24** .... for protection against bad air, known as **25** .... These were blamed for the spread of disease for hundreds of years, including epidemics of **26** .... in London and Paris in the middle of the 19th century.

READING PASSAGE 3

You should spend about 20 minutes on **Questions 27–40**, which are based on Reading Passage 3 on pages 47 and 48.

Questions 27–34

Reading Passage 3 has eight sections, **A–H**.

Choose the correct heading for each section from the list of headings below.

Write the correct number, *i–ix*, in boxes 27–34 on your answer sheet.

List of Headings

i	Complaints about the impact of a certain approach
ii	Fundamental beliefs that are in fact incorrect
iii	Early recommendations concerning business activities
iv	Organisations that put a new approach into practice
v	Companies that have suffered from changing their approach
vi	What people are increasingly expected to do
vii	How to achieve outcomes that are currently impossible
viii	Neither approach guarantees continuous improvement
ix	Evidence that a certain approach can have more disadvantages than advantages

---

27 Section **A**

28 Section **B**

29 Section **C**

30 Section **D**

31 Section **E**

32 Section **F**

33 Section **G**

34 Section **H**

Why companies should welcome disorder

A   Organisation is big business. Whether it is of our lives – all those inboxes and calendars – or how companies are structured, a multi-billion dollar industry helps to meet this need.

We have more strategies for time management, project management and self-organisation than at any other time in human history. We are told that we ought to organise our company, our home life, our week, our day and even our sleep, all as a means to becoming more productive. Every week, countless seminars and workshops take place around the world to tell a paying public that they ought to structure their lives in order to achieve this.

This rhetoric has also crept into the thinking of business leaders and entrepreneurs, much to the delight of self-proclaimed perfectionists with the need to get everything right. The number of business schools and graduates has massively increased over the past 50 years, essentially teaching people how to organise well.

B   Ironically, however, the number of businesses that fail has also steadily increased. Work-related stress has increased. A large proportion of workers from all demographics claim to be dissatisfied with the way their work is structured and the way they are managed.

This begs the question: what has gone wrong? Why is it that on paper the drive for organisation seems a sure shot for increasing productivity, but in reality falls well short of what is expected?

C   This has been a problem for a while now. Frederick Taylor was one of the forefathers of scientific management. Writing in the first half of the 20th century, he designed a number of principles to improve the efficiency of the work process, which have since become widespread in modern companies. So the approach has been around for a while.

D   New research suggests that this obsession with efficiency is misguided. The problem is not necessarily the management theories or strategies we use to organise our work; it's the basic assumptions we hold in approaching how we work. Here it's the assumption that order is a necessary condition for productivity. This assumption has also fostered the idea that disorder must be detrimental to organisational productivity. The result is that businesses and people spend time and money organising themselves for the sake of organising, rather than actually looking at the end goal and usefulness of such an effort.

E   What's more, recent studies show that order actually has diminishing returns. Order does increase productivity to a certain extent, but eventually the usefulness of the process of organisation, and the benefit it yields, reduce until the point where any further increase in order reduces productivity. Some argue that in a business, if the cost of formally structuring something outweighs the benefit of doing it, then that thing ought not to be formally structured. Instead, the resources involved can be better used elsewhere.

F In fact, research shows that, when innovating, the best approach is to create an environment devoid of structure and hierarchy and enable everyone involved to engage as one organic group. These environments can lead to new solutions that, under conventionally structured environments (filled with bottlenecks in terms of information flow, power structures, rules, and routines) would never be reached.

G In recent times companies have slowly started to embrace this disorganisation. Many of them embrace it in terms of perception (embracing the idea of disorder, as opposed to fearing it) and in terms of process (putting mechanisms in place to reduce structure).

For example, Oticon, a large Danish manufacturer of hearing aids, used what it called a 'spaghetti' structure in order to reduce the organisation's rigid hierarchies. This involved scrapping formal job titles and giving staff huge amounts of ownership over their own time and projects. This approach proved to be highly successful initially, with clear improvements in worker productivity in all facets of the business.

In similar fashion, the former chairman of General Electric embraced disorganisation, putting forward the idea of the 'boundaryless' organisation. Again, it involves breaking down the barriers between different parts of a company and encouraging virtual collaboration and flexible working. Google and a number of other tech companies have embraced (at least in part) these kinds of flexible structures, facilitated by technology and strong company values which glue people together.

H A word of warning to others thinking of jumping on this bandwagon: the evidence so far suggests disorder, much like order, also seems to have diminishing utility, and can also have detrimental effects on performance if overused. Like order, disorder should be embraced only so far as it is useful. But we should not fear it – nor venerate one over the other. This research also shows that we should continually question whether or not our existing assumptions work.

Questions 35–37

Complete the sentences below.

Choose ONE WORD ONLY from the passage for each answer.

Write your answers in boxes 35–37 on your answer sheet.

35 Numerous training sessions are aimed at people who feel they are not .... enough.

36 Being organised appeals to people who regard themselves as ....

37 Many people feel .... with aspects of their work.

Questions 38–40

Do the following statements agree with the information given in Reading Passage 3?

In boxes 38–40 on your answer sheet, write

TRUE	*if the statement agrees with the information*
FALSE	*if the statement contradicts the information*
NOT GIVEN	*if there is no information on this*

38 Both businesses and people aim at order without really considering its value.

39 Innovation is most successful if the people involved have distinct roles.

40 Google was inspired to adopt flexibility by the success of General Electric.

WRITING

WRITING TASK 1

You should spend about 20 minutes on this task.

The chart below shows the value of one country's exports in various categories during 2015 and 2016. The table shows the percentage change in each category of exports in 2016 compared with 2015.

Summarise the information by selecting and reporting the main features, and make comparisons where relevant.

Write at least 150 words.

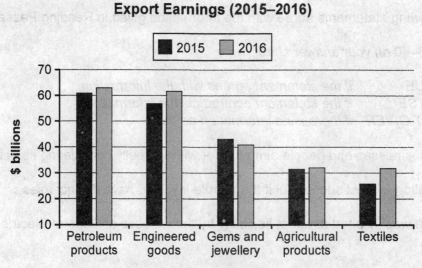

Export Earnings (2015–2016)

Percentage change in values (2015–2016)		
Petroleum products	⬆	3%
Engineered goods	⬆	8.5%
Gems and jewellery	⬇	5.18%
Agricultural products	⬆	0.81%
Textiles	⬆	15.24%

WRITING TASK 2

You should spend about 40 minutes on this task.

Write about the following topic:

> **Some people say that the main environmental problem of our time is the loss of particular species of plants and animals. Others say that there are more important environmental problems.**
>
> **Discuss both these views and give your own opinion.**

Give reasons for your answer and include any relevant examples from your own knowledge or experience.

Write at least 250 words.

SPEAKING

PART 1

The examiner asks the candidate about him/herself, his/her home, work or studies and other familiar topics.

EXAMPLE

Social media

- Which social media websites do you use?
- How much time do you spend on social media sites? [Why/Why not?]
- What kind of information about yourself have you put on social media? [Why/Why not?]
- Is there anything you don't like about social media? [Why?]

PART 2

Describe something you liked very much which you bought for your home.

You should say:
  what you bought
  when and where you bought it
  why you chose this particular thing

and explain why you liked it so much.

You will have to talk about the topic for one to two minutes. You have one minute to think about what you are going to say. You can make some notes to help you if you wish.

PART 3

Discussion topics:

Creating a nice home

Example questions:
Why do some people buy lots of things for their home?
Do you think it is very expensive to make a home look nice?
Why don't some people care about how their home looks?

Different types of home

Example questions:
In what ways is living in a flat/apartment better than living in a house?
Do you think homes will look different in the future?
Do you agree that the kinds of homes people prefer change as they get older?

Test 3

SECTION 1 — Questions 1–10

Complete the notes below.

Write **ONE WORD AND/OR A NUMBER** for each answer.

Flanders Conference Hotel

Example

Customer Services Manager: .... *Angela* ....

Date available
- weekend beginning February 4th

Conference facilities
- the **1** .... room for talks

   (projector and **2** .... available)
- area for coffee and an **3** ....
- free **4** .... throughout
- a standard buffet lunch costs **5** $ .... per head

Accommodation
- Rooms will cost **6** $ .... including breakfast.

Other facilities
- The hotel also has a spa and rooftop **7** ....
- There's a free shuttle service to the **8** ....

Location
- Wilby Street (quite near the **9** ....)
- near to restaurants and many **10** ....

SECTION 2   *Questions 11–20*

Questions 11 and 12

Choose TWO letters, A–E.

Which **TWO** activities that volunteers do are mentioned?

- **A**   decorating
- **B**   cleaning
- **C**   delivering meals
- **D**   shopping
- **E**   childcare

Questions 13 and 14

Choose TWO letters, A–E.

Which **TWO** ways that volunteers can benefit from volunteering are mentioned?

- **A**   learning how to be part of a team
- **B**   having a sense of purpose
- **C**   realising how lucky they are
- **D**   improved ability at time management
- **E**   boosting their employment prospects

Questions 15–20

What has each of the following volunteers helped someone to do?

*Choose **SIX** answers from the box and write the correct letter, **A–G**, next to Questions 15–20.*

What volunteers have helped people to do

A   overcome physical difficulties

B   rediscover skills not used for a long time

C   improve their communication skills

D   solve problems independently

E   escape isolation

F   remember past times

G   start a new hobby

Volunteers

15 Habib   ....

16 Consuela   ....

17 Minh   ....

18 Tanya   ....

19 Alexei   ....

20 Juba   ....

SECTION 3   *Questions 21–26*

Complete the notes below.

*Write **ONE WORD AND/OR A NUMBER** for each answer.*

Background on school marching band

It consists of around **21** .... students.

It is due to play in a **22** .... band competition.

It has been invited to play in the town's **23** ....

They have listened to a talk by a **24** ....

Joe will discuss a **25** .... with the band.

Joe hopes the band will attend a **26** .... next month.

Questions 27–30

What problem does Joe mention in connection with each of the following band members?

Choose **FOUR** *answers from the box and write the correct letter, A–F, next to Questions 27–30.*

> **Problems**
>
> A   makes a lot of mistakes in rehearsals
>
> B   keeps making unhelpful suggestions
>
> C   has difficulty with rhythm
>
> D   misses too many rehearsals
>
> E   has a health problem
>
> F   doesn't mix with other students

Band members

27   flautist   ....

28   trumpeter   ....

29   trombonist   ....

30   percussionist   ....

SECTION 4   Questions 31–40

Complete the notes below.

Write **ONE WORD AND/OR A NUMBER** for each answer.

Concerts in university arts festival

Concert 1

- Australian composer: Liza Lim

- studied piano and **31** .... before turning to composition

- performers and festivals around the world have given her a lot of commissions

- compositions show a great deal of **32** .... and are drawn from various cultural sources

- her music is very expressive and also **33** ....

- festival will include her **34** .... called *The Oresteia*

- Lim described the sounds in *The Oresteia* as **35** ....

- British composers: Ralph Vaughan Williams, Frederick Delius

Concert 2

- British composers: Benjamin Britten, Judith Weir

- Australian composer: Ross Edwards

- festival will include *The Tower of Remoteness*, inspired by nature

- *The Tower of Remoteness* is performed by piano and **36** ....

- compositions include music for children

- celebrates Australia's cultural **37** ....

Concert 3

- Australian composer: Carl Vine

- played cornet then piano

- studied **38** .... before studying music

- worked in Sydney as a pianist and composer

- became well known as composer of music for **39** ....

- festival will include his music for the 1996 **40** ....

- British composers: Edward Elgar, Thomas Adès

READING

READING PASSAGE 1

You should spend about 20 minutes on **Questions 1–13,** *which are based on Reading Passage 1 below.*

The concept of intelligence

A Looked at in one way, everyone knows what intelligence is; looked at in another way, no one does. In other words, people all have unconscious notions – known as 'implicit theories' – of intelligence, but no one knows for certain what it actually is. This chapter addresses how people conceptualize intelligence, whatever it may actually be.

But why should we even care what people think intelligence is, as opposed only to valuing whatever it actually is? There are at least four reasons people's conceptions of intelligence matter.

B First, implicit theories of intelligence drive the way in which people perceive and evaluate their own intelligence and that of others. To better understand the judgments people make about their own and others' abilities, it is useful to learn about people's implicit theories. For example, parents' implicit theories of their children's language development will determine at what ages they will be willing to make various corrections in their children's speech. More generally, parents' implicit theories of intelligence will determine at what ages they believe their children are ready to perform various cognitive tasks. Job interviewers will make hiring decisions on the basis of their implicit theories of intelligence. People will decide who to be friends with on the basis of such theories. In sum, knowledge about implicit theories of intelligence is important because this knowledge is so often used by people to make judgments in the course of their everyday lives.

C Second, the implicit theories of scientific investigators ultimately give rise to their explicit theories. Thus it is useful to find out what these implicit theories are. Implicit theories provide a framework that is useful in defining the general scope of a phenomenon – especially a not-well-understood phenomenon. These implicit theories can suggest what aspects of the phenomenon have been more or less attended to in previous investigations.

D Third, implicit theories can be useful when an investigator suspects that existing explicit theories are wrong or misleading. If an investigation of implicit theories reveals little correspondence between the extant implicit and explicit theories, the implicit theories may be wrong. But the possibility also needs to be taken into account that the explicit theories are wrong and in need of correction or supplementation. For example, some implicit theories of intelligence suggest the need for expansion of some of our explicit theories of the construct.

E   Finally, understanding implicit theories of intelligence can help elucidate developmental and cross-cultural differences. As mentioned earlier, people have expectations for intellectual performances that differ for children of different ages. How these expectations differ is in part a function of culture. For example, expectations for children who participate in Western-style schooling are almost certain to be different from those for children who do not participate in such schooling.

F   I have suggested that there are three major implicit theories of how intelligence relates to society as a whole (Sternberg, 1997). These might be called Hamiltonian, Jeffersonian, and Jacksonian. These views are not based strictly, but rather, loosely, on the philosophies of Alexander Hamilton, Thomas Jefferson, and Andrew Jackson, three great statesmen in the history of the United States.

G   The Hamiltonian view, which is similar to the Platonic view, is that people are born with different levels of intelligence and that those who are less intelligent need the good offices of the more intelligent to keep them in line, whether they are called government officials or, in Plato's term, philosopher-kings. Herrnstein and Murray (1994) seem to have shared this belief when they wrote about the emergence of a cognitive (high-IQ) elite, which eventually would have to take responsibility for the largely irresponsible masses of non-elite (low-IQ) people who cannot take care of themselves. Left to themselves, the unintelligent would create, as they always have created, a kind of chaos.

H   The Jeffersonian view is that people should have equal opportunities, but they do not necessarily avail themselves equally of these opportunities and are not necessarily equally rewarded for their accomplishments. People are rewarded for what they accomplish, if given equal opportunity. Low achievers are not rewarded to the same extent as high achievers. In the Jeffersonian view, the goal of education is not to favor or foster an elite, as in the Hamiltonian tradition, but rather to allow children the opportunities to make full use of the skills they have. My own views are similar to these (Sternberg, 1997).

I   The Jacksonian view is that all people are equal, not only as human beings but in terms of their competencies – that one person would serve as well as another in government or on a jury or in almost any position of responsibility. In this view of democracy, people are essentially intersubstitutable except for specialized skills, all of which can be learned. In this view, we do not need or want any institutions that might lead to favoring one group over another.

J   Implicit theories of intelligence and of the relationship of intelligence to society perhaps need to be considered more carefully than they have been because they often serve as underlying presuppositions for explicit theories and even experimental designs that are then taken as scientific contributions. Until scholars are able to discuss their implicit theories and thus their assumptions, they are likely to miss the point of what others are saying when discussing their explicit theories and their data.

Questions 1–3

Reading Passage 1 has ten sections, **A–J**.

Which section contains the following information?

*Write the correct letter, **A–J**, in boxes 1–3 on your answer sheet.*

1   information about how non-scientists' assumptions about intelligence influence their behaviour towards others

2   a reference to lack of clarity over the definition of intelligence

3   the point that a researcher's implicit and explicit theories may be very different

Questions 4–6

Do the following statements agree with the claims of the writer in Reading Passage 1?

In boxes 4–6 on your answer sheet, write

> **YES**   if the statement agrees with the claims of the writer
> **NO**   if the statement contradicts the claims of the writer
> **NOT GIVEN**   if it is impossible to say what the writer thinks about this

4   Slow language development in children is likely to prove disappointing to their parents.

5   People's expectations of what children should gain from education are universal.

6   Scholars may discuss theories without fully understanding each other.

Questions 7–13

Look at the following statements (Questions 7–13) and the list of theories below.

*Match each statement with the correct theory, **A**, **B**, or **C**.*

*Write the correct letter, **A**, **B**, or **C**, in boxes 7–13 on your answer sheet.*

NB *You may use any letter more than once.*

7   It is desirable for the same possibilities to be open to everyone.

8   No section of society should have preferential treatment at the expense of another.

9   People should only gain benefits on the basis of what they actually achieve.

10   Variation in intelligence begins at birth.

11   The more intelligent people should be in positions of power.

12   Everyone can develop the same abilities.

13   People of low intelligence are likely to lead uncontrolled lives.

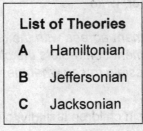

List of Theories

A   Hamiltonian

B   Jeffersonian

C   Jacksonian

READING PASSAGE 2

*You should spend about 20 minutes on **Questions 14–26**, which are based on Reading Passage 2 below.*

Saving bugs to find new drugs

Zoologist Ross Piper looks at the potential of insects in pharmaceutical research

A   More drugs than you might think are derived from, or inspired by, compounds found in living things. Looking to nature for the soothing and curing of our ailments is nothing new – we have been doing it for tens of thousands of years. You only have to look at other primates – such as the capuchin monkeys who rub themselves with toxin-oozing millipedes to deter mosquitoes, or the chimpanzees who use noxious forest plants to rid themselves of intestinal parasites – to realise that our ancient ancestors too probably had a basic grasp of medicine.

B   Pharmaceutical science and chemistry built on these ancient foundations and perfected the extraction, characterisation, modification and testing of these natural products. Then, for a while, modern pharmaceutical science moved its focus away from nature and into the laboratory, designing chemical compounds from scratch. The main cause of this shift is that although there are plenty of promising chemical compounds in nature, finding them is far from easy. Securing sufficient numbers of the organism in question, isolating and characterising the compounds of interest, and producing large quantities of these compounds are all significant hurdles.

C   Laboratory-based drug discovery has achieved varying levels of success, something which has now prompted the development of new approaches focusing once again on natural products. With the ability to mine genomes for useful compounds, it is now evident that we have barely scratched the surface of nature's molecular diversity. This realisation, together with several looming health crises, such as antibiotic resistance, has put bioprospecting – the search for useful compounds in nature – firmly back on the map.

D   Insects are the undisputed masters of the terrestrial domain, where they occupy every possible niche. Consequently, they have a bewildering array of interactions with other organisms, something which has driven the evolution of an enormous range of very interesting compounds for defensive and offensive purposes. Their remarkable diversity exceeds that of every other group of animals on the planet combined. Yet even though insects are far and away the most diverse animals in existence, their potential as sources of therapeutic compounds is yet to be realised.

E   From the tiny proportion of insects that have been investigated, several promising compounds have been identified. For example, alloferon, an antimicrobial compound produced by blow fly larvae, is used as an antiviral and antitumor agent in South Korea and Russia. The larvae of a few other insect species are being investigated for the potent antimicrobial compounds they produce. Meanwhile, a compound from the venom of the wasp *Polybia paulista* has potential in cancer treatment.

F   Why is it that insects have received relatively little attention in bioprospecting? Firstly, there are so many insects that, without some manner of targeted approach, investigating this huge variety of species is a daunting task. Secondly, insects are generally very small, and the glands inside them that secrete potentially useful compounds are smaller still. This can make it difficult to obtain sufficient quantities of the compound for subsequent testing. Thirdly, although we consider insects to be everywhere, the reality of this ubiquity is vast numbers of a few extremely common species. Many insect species are infrequently encountered and very difficult to rear in captivity, which, again, can leave us with insufficient material to work with.

G   My colleagues and I at Aberystwyth University in the UK have developed an approach in which we use our knowledge of ecology as a guide to target our efforts. The creatures that particularly interest us are the many insects that secrete powerful poison for subduing prey and keeping it fresh for future consumption. There are even more insects that are masters of exploiting filthy habitats, such as faeces and carcasses, where they are regularly challenged by thousands of micro-organisms. These insects have many antimicrobial compounds for dealing with pathogenic bacteria and fungi, suggesting that there is certainly potential to find many compounds that can serve as or inspire new antibiotics.

H   Although natural history knowledge points us in the right direction, it doesn't solve the problems associated with obtaining useful compounds from insects. Fortunately, it is now possible to snip out the stretches of the insect's DNA that carry the codes for the interesting compounds and insert them into cell lines that allow larger quantities to be produced. And although the road from isolating and characterising compounds with desirable qualities to developing a commercial product is very long and full of pitfalls, the variety of successful animal-derived pharmaceuticals on the market demonstrates there is a precedent here that is worth exploring.

I   With every bit of wilderness that disappears, we deprive ourselves of potential medicines. As much as I'd love to help develop a groundbreaking insect-derived medicine, my main motivation for looking at insects in this way is conservation. I sincerely believe that all species, however small and seemingly insignificant, have a right to exist for their own sake. If we can shine a light on the darker recesses of nature's medicine cabinet, exploring the useful chemistry of the most diverse animals on the planet, I believe we can make people think differently about the value of nature.

Questions 14–20

Reading Passage 2 has nine paragraphs, **A–I**.

Which paragraph contains the following information?

*Write the correct letter, **A–I**, in boxes 14–20 on your answer sheet.*

14   mention of factors driving a renewed interest in natural medicinal compounds

15   how recent technological advances have made insect research easier

16   examples of animals which use medicinal substances from nature

17   reasons why it is challenging to use insects in drug research

18   reference to how interest in drug research may benefit wildlife

19   a reason why nature-based medicines fell out of favour for a period

20   an example of an insect-derived medicine in use at the moment

Questions 21 and 22

*Choose **TWO** letters, **A–E**.*

Write the correct letters in boxes 21 and 22 on your answer sheet.

Which **TWO** of the following make insects interesting for drug research?

    A   the huge number of individual insects in the world
    B   the variety of substances insects have developed to protect themselves
    C   the potential to extract and make use of insects' genetic codes
    D   the similarities between different species of insect
    E   the manageable size of most insects

Questions 23–26

Complete the summary below.

Choose **ONE WORD ONLY** from the passage for each answer.

Write your answers in boxes 23–26 on your answer sheet.

Research at Aberystwyth University

Ross Piper and fellow zoologists at Aberystwyth University are using their expertise in **23** .... when undertaking bioprospecting with insects. They are especially interested in the compounds that insects produce to overpower and preserve their **24** .... They are also interested in compounds which insects use to protect themselves from pathogenic bacteria and fungi found in their **25** .... Piper hopes that these substances will be useful in the development of drugs such as **26** ....

READING PASSAGE 3

*You should spend about 20 minutes on **Questions 27–40**, which are based on Reading Passage 3 below.*

The power of play

Virtually every child, the world over, plays. The drive to play is so intense that children will do so in any circumstances, for instance when they have no real toys, or when parents do not actively encourage the behavior. In the eyes of a young child, running, pretending, and building are fun. Researchers and educators know that these playful activities benefit the development of the whole child across social, cognitive, physical, and emotional domains. Indeed, play is such an instrumental component to healthy child development that the United Nations High Commission on Human Rights (1989) recognized play as a fundamental right of every child.

Yet, while experts continue to expound a powerful argument for the importance of play in children's lives, the actual time children spend playing continues to decrease. Today, children play eight hours less each week than their counterparts did two decades ago (Elkind 2008). Under pressure of rising academic standards, play is being replaced by test preparation in kindergartens and grade schools, and parents who aim to give their preschoolers a leg up are led to believe that flashcards and educational 'toys' are the path to success. Our society has created a false dichotomy between play and learning.

Through play, children learn to regulate their behavior, lay the foundations for later learning in science and mathematics, figure out the complex negotiations of social relationships, build a repertoire of creative problem-solving skills, and so much more. There is also an important role for adults in guiding children through playful learning opportunities.

Full consensus on a formal definition of play continues to elude the researchers and theorists who study it. Definitions range from discrete descriptions of various types of play such as physical, construction, language, or symbolic play (Miller & Almon 2009), to lists of broad criteria, based on observations and attitudes, that are meant to capture the essence of all play behaviors (e.g. Rubin et al. 1983).

A majority of the contemporary definitions of play focus on several key criteria. The founder of the National Institute for Play, Stuart Brown, has described play as 'anything that spontaneously is done for its own sake'. More specifically, he says it 'appears purposeless, produces pleasure and joy, [and] leads one to the next stage of mastery' (as quoted in Tippett 2008). Similarly, Miller and Almon (2009) say that play includes 'activities that are freely chosen and directed by children and arise from intrinsic motivation'. Often, play is defined along a continuum as more or less playful using the following set of behavioral and dispositional criteria (e.g. Rubin et al. 1983):

Play is pleasurable: Children must enjoy the activity or it is not play. It is intrinsically motivated: Children engage in play simply for the satisfaction the behavior itself brings. It has no extrinsically motivated function or goal. Play is process oriented: When children play, the means are more important than the ends. It is freely chosen, spontaneous and voluntary. If a child is pressured, they will likely not think of the activity as play. Play is actively engaged: Players must be physically and/or mentally involved in the activity. Play is non-literal. It involves make-believe.

According to this view, children's playful behaviors can range in degree from 0% to 100% playful. Rubin and colleagues did not assign greater weight to any one dimension in determining playfulness; however, other researchers have suggested that process orientation and a lack of obvious functional purpose may be the most important aspects of play (e.g. Pellegrini 2009).

From the perspective of a continuum, play can thus blend with other motives and attitudes that are less playful, such as work. Unlike play, work is typically not viewed as enjoyable and it is extrinsically motivated (i.e. it is goal oriented). Researcher Joan Goodman (1994) suggested that hybrid forms of work and play are not a detriment to learning; rather, they can provide optimal contexts for learning. For example, a child may be engaged in a difficult, goal-directed activity set up by their teacher, but they may still be actively engaged and intrinsically motivated. At this mid-point between play and work, the child's motivation, coupled with guidance from an adult, can create robust opportunities for playful learning.

Critically, recent research supports the idea that adults can facilitate children's learning while maintaining a playful approach in interactions known as 'guided play' (Fisher et al. 2011). The adult's role in play varies as a function of their educational goals and the child's developmental level (Hirsch-Pasek et al. 2009).

Guided play takes two forms. At a very basic level, adults can enrich the child's environment by providing objects or experiences that promote aspects of a curriculum. In the more direct form of guided play, parents or other adults can support children's play by joining in the fun as a co-player, raising thoughtful questions, commenting on children's discoveries, or encouraging further exploration or new facets to the child's activity. Although playful learning can be somewhat structured, it must also be child-centered (Nicolopolou et al. 2006). Play should stem from the child's own desire.

Both free and guided play are essential elements in a child-centered approach to playful learning. Intrinsically motivated free play provides the child with true autonomy, while guided play is an avenue through which parents and educators can provide more targeted learning experiences. In either case, play should be actively engaged, it should be predominantly child-directed, and it must be fun.

Questions 27–31

Look at the following statements (Questions 27–31) and the list of researchers below.

*Match each statement with the correct researcher, **A–G**.*

*Write the correct letter, **A–G**, in boxes 27–31 on your answer sheet.*

27   Play can be divided into a number of separate categories.

28   Adults' intended goals affect how they play with children.

29   Combining work with play may be the best way for children to learn.

30   Certain elements of play are more significant than others.

31   Activities can be classified on a scale of playfulness.

List of Researchers

A   Elkind

B   Miller & Almon

C   Rubin et al.

D   Stuart Brown

E   Pellegrini

F   Joan Goodman

G   Hirsch-Pasek et al.

Questions 32–36

Do the following statements agree with the claims of the writer in Reading Passage 3?

In boxes 32–36 on your answer sheet, write

YES	if the statement agrees with the claims of the writer
NO	if the statement contradicts the claims of the writer
NOT GIVEN	if it is impossible to say what the writer thinks about this

32 Children need toys in order to play.

33 It is a mistake to treat play and learning as separate types of activities.

34 Play helps children to develop their artistic talents.

35 Researchers have agreed on a definition of play.

36 Work and play differ in terms of whether or not they have a target.

Questions 37–40

Complete the summary below.

*Choose **ONE WORD ONLY** from the passage for each answer.*

Write your answers in boxes 37–40 on your answer sheet.

Guided play

In the simplest form of guided play, an adult contributes to the environment in which the child is playing. Alternatively, an adult can play with a child and develop the play, for instance by 37 .... the child to investigate different aspects of their game. Adults can help children to learn through play, and may make the activity rather structured, but it should still be based on the child's 38 .... to play.

Play without the intervention of adults gives children real 39 .... ; with adults, play can be 40 .... at particular goals. However, all forms of play should be an opportunity for children to have fun.

WRITING

WRITING TASK 1

You should spend about 20 minutes on this task.

> **The diagram below shows how electricity is generated in a hydroelectric power station.**
>
> **Summarise the information by selecting and reporting the main features, and make comparisons where relevant.**

Write at least 150 words.

Hydroelectric power station

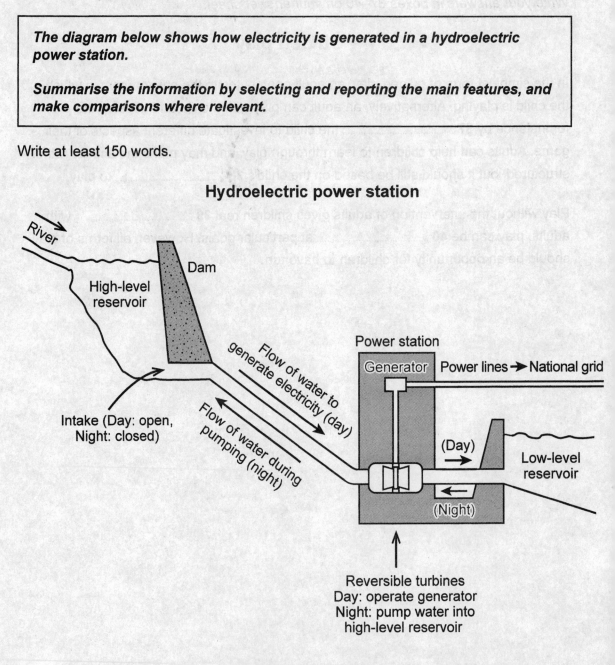

WRITING TASK 2

You should spend about 40 minutes on this task.

Write about the following topic:

> **Some people say that music is a good way of bringing people of different cultures and ages together.**
>
> **To what extent do you agree or disagree with this opinion?**

Give reasons for your answer and include any relevant examples from your own knowledge or experience.

Write at least 250 words.

SPEAKING

PART 1

The examiner asks the candidate about him/herself, his/her home, **work** or studies and other familiar topics.

EXAMPLE

Neighbours

• How often do you see your neighbours? [Why/Why not?]
• Do you invite your neighbours to your home? [Why/Why not?]
• Do you think you are a good neighbour? [Why/Why not?]
• Has a neighbour ever helped you? [Why/Why not?]

PART 2

Describe a very difficult task that you succeeded in doing as part of your work or studies. **You should say:** 　　**what task you did** 　　**why this task was very difficult** 　　**how you worked on this task** **and explain how you felt when you had successfully completed this task.**

You will have to talk about the topic for one to two minutes. You have one minute to think about what you are going to say. You can make some notes to help you if you wish.

PART 3

Discussion topics:

Difficult jobs

Example questions:
What are the most difficult jobs that people do?
Why do you think some people choose to do difficult jobs?
Do you agree or disagree that all jobs are difficult sometimes?

Personal and career success

Example questions:
How important is it for everyone to have a goal in their personal life?
Is it always necessary to work hard in order to achieve career success?
Do you think that successful people are always happy people?

Test 4

SECTION 1   Questions 1–10

Questions 1–7

Complete the notes below.

*Write **ONE WORD AND/OR A NUMBER** for each answer.*

Enquiry about booking hotel room for event

Example

Andrew is the ....*Events*............. Manager

Rooms

Adelphi Room
  number of people who can sit down to eat: 1 ....
  has a gallery suitable for musicians
  can go out and see the 2 .... in pots on the terrace
  terrace has a view of a group of 3 ....

Carlton Room
  number of people who can sit down to eat: 110
  has a 4 ....
  view of the lake

Options

Master of Ceremonies:
  can give a 5 .... while people are eating
  will provide 6 .... if there are any problems

Accommodation:
  in hotel rooms or 7 ....

Questions 8–10

What is said about using each of the following hotel facilities?

Choose **THREE** answers from the box and write the correct letter, *A, B* or *C*, next to Questions 8–10.

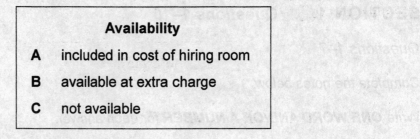

Availability
A included in cost of hiring room
B available at extra charge
C not available

Hotel facilities

8   outdoor swimming pool   ....

9   gym   ....

10 tennis courts   ....

SECTION 2   *Questions 11–20*

Questions 11–16

What information does the speaker give about each of the following excursions?

*Choose **SIX** answers from the box and write the correct letter, **A–H**, next to Questions 11–16.*

> **Information**
>
> A   all downhill
>
> B   suitable for beginners
>
> C   only in good weather
>
> D   food included
>
> E   no charge
>
> F   swimming possible
>
> G   fully booked today
>
> H   transport not included

Excursions

11   dolphin watching   ....

12   forest walk   ....

13   cycle trip   ....

14   local craft tour   ....

15   observatory trip   ....

16   horse riding   ....

Test 4

Questions 17 and 18

Choose TWO letters, A–E.

Which TWO things does the speaker say about the attraction called *Musical Favourites*?

A   You pay extra for drinks.
B   You must book it in advance.
C   You get a reduction if you buy two tickets.
D   You can meet the performers.
E   You can take part in the show.

Questions 19 and 20

Choose TWO letters, A–E.

Which TWO things does the speaker say about the *Castle Feast*?

A   Visitors can dance after the meal.
B   There is a choice of food.
C   Visitors wear historical costume.
D   Knives and forks are not used.
E   The entertainment includes horse races.

SECTION 3   *Questions 21–30*

Questions 21–25

Choose the correct letter, A, B or C.

21 What does Trevor find interesting about the purpose of children's literature?

    A   the fact that authors may not realise what values they're teaching
    B   the fact that literature can be entertaining and educational at the same time
    C   the fact that adults expect children to imitate characters in literature

22 Trevor says the module about the purpose of children's literature made him

    A   analyse some of the stories that his niece reads.
    B   wonder how far popularity reflects good quality.
    C   decide to start writing some children's stories.

23 Stephanie is interested in the Pictures module because

    A   she intends to become an illustrator.
    B   she can remember beautiful illustrations from her childhood.
    C   she believes illustrations are more important than words.

24 Trevor and Stephanie agree that comics

    A   are inferior to books.
    B   have the potential for being useful.
    C   discourage children from using their imagination.

25 With regard to books aimed at only boys or only girls, Trevor was surprised

    A   how long the distinction had gone unquestioned.
    B   how few books were aimed at both girls and boys.
    C   how many children enjoyed books intended for the opposite sex.

Test 4

Questions 26–30

What comment is made about each of these stories?

Choose **FIVE** answers from the box and write the correct letter, **A–G**, next to Questions 26–30.

```
                       Comments

A    translated into many other languages

B    hard to read

C    inspired a work in a different area of art

D    more popular than the author's other works

E    original title refers to another book

F    started a new genre

G    unlikely topic
```

Stories

26 Perrault's fairy tales   ....

27 *The Swiss Family Robinson*   ....

28 *The Nutcracker and The Mouse King* ....

29 *The Lord of the Rings*   ....

30 *War Horse*   ....

SECTION 4   *Questions 31–40*

Complete the notes below.

Write ONE WORD ONLY for each answer.

The hunt for sunken settlements and ancient shipwrecks

ATLIT-YAM

- was a village on coast of eastern Mediterranean
- thrived until about 7,000 BC
- stone homes had a courtyard
- had a semicircle of large stones round a **31** ....
- cause of destruction unknown – now under the sea
- biggest settlement from the prehistoric period found on the seabed
- research carried out into structures, **32** .... and human remains

TRADITIONAL AUTONOMOUS UNDERWATER VEHICLES (AUVs)

- used in the oil industry, e.g. to make **33** ....
- problems: they were expensive and **34** ....

LATEST AUVs

- much easier to use, relatively cheap, sophisticated

Tests:

- Marzamemi, Sicily: found ancient Roman ships carrying architectural elements made of **35** ....

Underwater internet:

- **36** .... is used for short distance communication, acoustic waves for long distance
- plans for communication with researchers by satellite
- AUV can send data to another AUV that has better **37** ...., for example

Planned research in Gulf of Baratti:

- to find out more about wrecks of ancient Roman ships, including

    – one carrying **38** .... supplies; tablets may have been used for cleaning the **39** ....

    – others carrying containers of olive oil or **40** ....

READING PASSAGE 1

*You should spend about 20 minutes on **Questions 1–13,** which are based on Reading Passage 1 below.*

The secret of staying young

Pheidole dentata, a native ant of the south-eastern U.S., isn't immortal. But scientists have found that it doesn't seem to show any signs of aging. Old worker ants can do everything just as well as the youngsters, and their brains appear just as sharp. 'We get a picture that these ants really don't decline,' says Ysabel Giraldo, who studied the ants for her doctoral thesis at Boston University.

Such age-defying feats are rare in the animal kingdom. Naked mole rats can live for almost 30 years and stay fit for nearly their entire lives. They can still reproduce even when old, and they never get cancer. But the vast majority of animals deteriorate with age just like people do. Like the naked mole rat, ants are social creatures that usually live in highly organised colonies. 'It's this social complexity that makes *P. dentata* useful for studying aging in people,' says Giraldo, now at the California Institute of Technology. Humans are also highly social, a trait that has been connected to healthier aging. By contrast, most animal studies of aging use mice, worms or fruit flies, which all lead much more isolated lives.

In the lab, *P. dentata* worker ants typically live for around 140 days. Giraldo focused on ants at four age ranges: 20 to 22 days, 45 to 47 days, 95 to 97 days and 120 to 122 days. Unlike all previous studies, which only estimated how old the ants were, her work tracked the ants from the time the pupae became adults, so she knew their exact ages. Then she put them through a range of tests.

Giraldo watched how well the ants took care of the young of the colony, recording how often each ant attended to, carried and fed them. She compared how well 20-day-old and 95-day-old ants followed the telltale scent that the insects usually leave to mark a trail to food. She tested how ants responded to light and also measured how active they were by counting how often ants in a small dish walked across a line. And she experimented with how ants react to live prey: a tethered fruit fly. Giraldo expected the older ants to perform poorly in all these tasks. But the elderly insects were all good caretakers and trail-followers—the 95-day-old ants could track the scent even longer than their younger counterparts. They all responded to light well, and the older ants were more active. And when it came to reacting to prey, the older ants attacked the poor fruit fly just as aggressively as the young ones did, flaring their mandibles or pulling at the fly's legs.

Then Giraldo compared the brains of 20-day-old and 95-day-old ants, identifying any cells that were close to death. She saw no major differences with age, nor was there any difference in the location of the dying cells, showing that age didn't seem to affect specific brain functions. Ants and other insects have structures in their brains called mushroom bodies, which are important for processing information, learning and memory. She also wanted to see if aging affects the density of synaptic complexes within these structures—regions where neurons come together. Again, the answer was no. What was more, the old ants didn't experience any drop in the levels of either serotonin or dopamine—brain chemicals whose decline often coincides with aging. In humans, for example, a decrease in serotonin has been linked to Alzheimer's disease.

'This is the first time anyone has looked at both behavioral and neural changes in these ants so thoroughly,' says Giraldo, who recently published the findings in the *Proceedings of the Royal Society B*. Scientists have looked at some similar aspects in bees, but the results of recent bee studies were mixed—some studies showed age-related declines, which biologists call senescence, and others didn't. 'For now, the study raises more questions than it answers,' Giraldo says, 'including how *P. dentata* stays in such good shape.'

Also, if the ants don't deteriorate with age, why do they die at all? Out in the wild, the ants probably don't live for a full 140 days thanks to predators, disease and just being in an environment that's much harsher than the comforts of the lab. 'The lucky ants that do live into old age may suffer a steep decline just before dying,' Giraldo says, but she can't say for sure because her study wasn't designed to follow an ant's final moments.

'It will be important to extend these findings to other species of social insects,' says Gene E. Robinson, an entomologist at the University of Illinois at Urbana-Champaign. This ant might be unique, or it might represent a broader pattern among other social bugs with possible clues to the science of aging in larger animals. Either way, it seems that for these ants, age really doesn't matter.

Questions 1–8

Complete the notes below.

Choose **ONE WORD ONLY** from the passage for each answer.

Write your answer in boxes 1–8 on your answer sheet.

Ysabel Giraldo's research

Focused on a total of **1** .... different age groups of ants, analysing

Behaviour:

* how well ants looked after their **2** ....

* their ability to locate **3** .... using a scent trail

* the effect that **4** .... had on them

* how **5** .... they attacked prey

Brains:

* comparison between age and the **6** .... of dying cells in the brains of ants

* condition of synaptic complexes (areas in which **7** .... meet) in the brain's 'mushroom bodies'

* level of two **8** .... in the brain associated with ageing

---

Questions 9–13

Do the following statements agree with the information given in Reading Passage 1?

In boxes 9–13 on your answer sheet, write

> **TRUE**   if the statement agrees with the information
> **FALSE**   if the statement contradicts the information
> **NOT GIVEN**   if there is no information on this

9   *Pheidole dentata* ants are the only known animals which remain active for almost their whole lives.

10   Ysabel Giraldo was the first person to study *Pheidole dentata* ants using precise data about the insects' ages.

11   The ants in Giraldo's experiments behaved as she had predicted that they would.

12   The recent studies of bees used different methods of measuring age-related decline.

13   *Pheidole dentata* ants kept in laboratory conditions tend to live longer lives.

READING PASSAGE 2

*You should spend about 20 minutes on **Questions 14–26**, which are based on Reading Passage 2 below.*

Why zoos are good

Scientist David Hone makes the case for zoos

A   In my view, it is perfectly possible for many species of animals living in zoos or wildlife parks to have a quality of life as high as, or higher than, in the wild. Animals in good zoos get a varied and high-quality diet with all the supplements required, and any illnesses they might have will be treated. Their movement might be somewhat restricted, but they have a safe environment in which to live, and they are spared bullying and social ostracism by others of their kind. They do not suffer from the threat or stress of predators, or the irritation and pain of parasites or injuries. The average captive animal will have a greater life expectancy compared with its wild counterpart, and will not die of drought, of starvation or in the jaws of a predator. A lot of very nasty things happen to truly 'wild' animals that simply don't happen in good zoos, and to view a life that is 'free' as one that is automatically 'good' is, I think, an error. Furthermore, zoos serve several key purposes.

B   Firstly, zoos aid conservation. Colossal numbers of species are becoming extinct across the world, and many more are increasingly threatened and therefore risk extinction. Moreover, some of these collapses have been sudden, dramatic and unexpected, or were simply discovered very late in the day. A species protected in captivity can be bred up to provide a reservoir population against a population crash or extinction in the wild. A good number of species only exist in captivity, with many of these living in zoos. Still more only exist in the wild because they have been reintroduced from zoos, or have wild populations that have been boosted by captive bred animals. Without these efforts there would be fewer species alive today. Although reintroduction successes are few and far between, the numbers are increasing, and the very fact that species have been saved or reintroduced as a result of captive breeding proves the value of such initiatives.

C   Zoos also provide education. Many children and adults, especially those in cities, will never see a wild animal beyond a fox or pigeon. While it is true that television documentaries are becoming ever more detailed and impressive, and many natural history specimens are on display in museums, there really is nothing to compare with seeing a living creature in the flesh, hearing it, smelling it, watching what it does and having the time to absorb details. That alone will bring a greater understanding and perspective to many, and hopefully give them a greater appreciation for wildlife, conservation efforts and how they can contribute.

D   In addition to this, there is also the education that can take place in zoos through signs, talks and presentations which directly communicate information to visitors about the animals they are seeing and their place in the world. This was an area where zoos used to be lacking, but they are now increasingly sophisticated in their communication and outreach work. Many zoos also work directly to educate conservation workers in other countries, or send their animal keepers abroad to contribute their knowledge and skills to those working in zoos and reserves, thereby helping to improve conditions and reintroductions all over the world.

E   Zoos also play a key role in research. If we are to save wild species and restore and repair ecosystems we need to know about how key species live, act and react. Being able to undertake research on animals in zoos where there is less risk and fewer variables means real changes can be effected on wild populations. Finding out about, for example, the oestrus cycle of an animal or its breeding rate helps us manage wild populations. Procedures such as capturing and moving at-risk or dangerous individuals are bolstered by knowledge gained in zoos about doses for anaesthetics, and by experience in handling and transporting animals. This can make a real difference to conservation efforts and to the reduction of human–animal conflicts, and can provide a knowledge base for helping with the increasing threats of habitat destruction and other problems.

F   In conclusion, considering the many ongoing global threats to the environment, it is hard for me to see zoos as anything other than essential to the long-term survival of numerous species. They are vital not just in terms of protecting animals, but as a means of learning about them to aid those still in the wild, as well as educating and informing the general population about these animals and their world so that they can assist or at least accept the need to be more environmentally conscious. Without them, the world would be, and would increasingly become, a much poorer place.

Questions 14–17

Reading Passage 2 has six paragraphs, **A–F**.

Which paragraph contains the following information?

*Write the correct letter, **A–F**, in boxes 14–17 on your answer sheet.*

14 a reference to how quickly animal species can die out

15 reasons why it is preferable to study animals in captivity rather than in the wild

16 mention of two ways of learning about animals other than visiting them in zoos

17 reasons why animals in zoos may be healthier than those in the wild

Questions 18–22

Do the following statements agree with the information given in Reading Passage 2?

In boxes 18–22 on your answer sheet, write

> **TRUE**　　　*if the statement agrees with the information*
> **FALSE**　　*if the statement contradicts the information*
> **NOT GIVEN**　*if there is no information on this*

18 An animal is likely to live longer in a zoo than in the wild.

19 There are some species in zoos which can no longer be found in the wild.

20 Improvements in the quality of TV wildlife documentaries have resulted in increased numbers of zoo visitors.

21 Zoos have always excelled at transmitting information about animals to the public.

22 Studying animals in zoos is less stressful for the animals than studying them in the wild.

Questions 23 and 24

Choose TWO letters, A–E.

Write the correct letters in boxes 23 and 24 on your answer sheet.

Which **TWO** of the following are stated about zoo staff in the text?

- **A** Some take part in television documentaries about animals.
- **B** Some travel to overseas locations to join teams in zoos.
- **C** Some get experience with species in the wild before taking up zoo jobs.
- **D** Some teach people who are involved with conservation projects.
- **E** Some specialise in caring for species which are under threat.

Questions 25 and 26

Choose TWO letters, A–E.

Write the correct letters in boxes 25 and 26 on your answer sheet.

Which **TWO** of these beliefs about zoos does the writer mention in the text?

- **A** They can help children overcome their fears of wild animals.
- **B** They can increase public awareness of environmental issues.
- **C** They can provide employment for a range of professional people.
- **D** They can generate income to support wildlife conservation projects.
- **E** They can raise animals which can later be released into the wild.

READING PASSAGE 3

You should spend about 20 minutes on **Questions 27–40**, which are based on Reading Passage 3 below.

Chelsea Rochman, an ecologist at the University of California, Davis, has been trying to answer a dismal question: Is everything terrible, or are things just very, very bad?

Rochman is a member of the National Center for Ecological Analysis and Synthesis's marine-debris working group, a collection of scientists who study, among other things, the growing problem of marine debris, also known as ocean trash. Plenty of studies have sounded alarm bells about the state of marine debris; in a recent paper published in the journal *Ecology*, Rochman and her colleagues set out to determine how many of those perceived risks are real.

Often, Rochman says, scientists will end a paper by speculating about the broader impacts of what they've found. For example, a study could show that certain seabirds eat plastic bags, and go on to warn that whole bird populations are at risk of dying out. 'But the truth was that nobody had yet tested those perceived threats,' Rochman says. 'There wasn't a lot of information.'

Rochman and her colleagues examined more than a hundred papers on the impacts of marine debris that were published through 2013. Within each paper, they asked what threats scientists had studied – 366 perceived threats in all – and what they'd actually found.

In 83 percent of cases, the perceived dangers of ocean trash were proven true. In the remaining cases, the working group found the studies had weaknesses in design and content which affected the validity of their conclusions – they lacked a control group, for example, or used faulty statistics.

Strikingly, Rochman says, only one well-designed study failed to find the effect it was looking for, an investigation of mussels ingesting microscopic plastic bits. The plastic moved from the mussels' stomachs to their bloodstreams, scientists found, and stayed there for weeks – but didn't seem to stress out the shellfish.

While mussels may be fine eating trash, though, the analysis also gave a clearer picture of the many ways that ocean debris *is* bothersome.

Within the studies they looked at, most of the proven threats came from plastic debris, rather than other materials like metal or wood. Most of the dangers also involved large pieces of debris – animals getting entangled in trash, for example, or eating it and severely injuring themselves.

But a lot of ocean debris is 'microplastic', or pieces smaller than five millimeters. These may be ingredients used in cosmetics and toiletries, fibers shed by synthetic clothing in the wash, or eroded remnants of larger debris. Compared to the number of studies investigating large-scale debris, Rochman's group found little research on the effects of these tiny bits. 'There are a lot of open questions still for microplastic,' Rochman says, though she notes that more papers on the subject have been published since 2013, the cutoff point for the group's analysis.

There are also, she adds, a lot of open questions about the ways that ocean debris can lead to sea-creature death. Many studies have looked at how plastic affects an individual animal, or that animal's tissues or cells, rather than whole populations. And in the lab, scientists often use higher concentrations of plastic than what's really in the ocean. None of that tells us how many birds or fish or sea turtles could die from plastic pollution – or how deaths in one species could affect that animal's predators, or the rest of the ecosystem.

'We need to be asking more ecologically relevant questions,' Rochman says. Usually, scientists don't know exactly how disasters such as a tanker accidentally spilling its whole cargo of oil and polluting huge areas of the ocean will affect the environment until after they've happened. 'We don't ask the right questions early enough,' she says. But if ecologists can understand how the slow-moving effect of ocean trash is damaging ecosystems, they might be able to prevent things from getting worse.

Asking the right questions can help policy makers, and the public, figure out where to focus their attention. The problems that look or sound most dramatic may not be the best places to start. For example, the name of the 'Great Pacific Garbage Patch' – a collection of marine debris in the northern Pacific Ocean – might conjure up a vast, floating trash island. In reality though, much of the debris is tiny or below the surface; a person could sail through the area without seeing any trash at all. A Dutch group called 'The Ocean Cleanup' is currently working on plans to put mechanical devices in the Pacific Garbage Patch and similar areas to suck up plastic. But a recent paper used simulations to show that strategically positioning the cleanup devices closer to shore would more effectively reduce pollution over the long term.

'I think clearing up some of these misperceptions is really important,' Rochman says. Among scientists as well as in the media, she says, 'A lot of the images about strandings and entanglement and all of that cause the perception that plastic debris is killing everything in the ocean.' Interrogating the existing scientific literature can help ecologists figure out which problems really need addressing, and which ones they'd be better off – like the mussels – absorbing and ignoring.

Questions 27–33

Do the following statements agree with the information given in Reading Passage 3?

In boxes 27–33 on your answer sheet, write

> **TRUE**　　　　*if the statement agrees with the information*
> **FALSE**　　　*if the statement contradicts the information*
> **NOT GIVEN**　*if there is no information on this*

27　Rochman and her colleagues were the first people to research the problem of marine debris.

28　The creatures most in danger from ocean trash are certain seabirds.

29　The studies Rochman has reviewed have already proved that populations of some birds will soon become extinct.

30　Rochman analysed papers on the different kinds of danger caused by ocean trash.

31　Most of the research analysed by Rochman and her colleagues was badly designed.

32　One study examined by Rochman was expecting to find that mussels were harmed by eating plastic.

33　Some mussels choose to eat plastic in preference to their natural diet.

Questions 34–39

Complete the notes below.

*Choose **ONE WORD ONLY** from the passage for each answer.*

Write your answers in boxes 34–39 on your answer sheet.

Findings related to marine debris

Studies of marine debris found the biggest threats were

- plastic (not metal or wood)
- bits of debris that were **34** .... (harmful to animals)

There was little research into **35** .... e.g. from synthetic fibres.

Drawbacks of the studies examined

- most of them focused on individual animals, not entire **36** ....
- the **37** .... of plastic used in the lab did not always reflect those in the ocean
- there was insufficient information on
  - numbers of animals which could be affected
  - the impact of a reduction in numbers on the **38** .... of that species
  - the impact on the ecosystem

Rochman says more information is needed on the possible impact of future **39** .... (e.g. involving oil).

Question 40

*Choose the correct letter, **A, B, C** or **D**.*

Write the correct letter in box 40 on your answer sheet.

40   What would be the best title for this passage?

    A   Assessing the threat of marine debris
    B   Marine debris: who is to blame?
    C   A new solution to the problem of marine debris
    D   Marine debris: the need for international action

WRITING

WRITING TASK 1

You should spend about 20 minutes on this task.

> *The plans below show a public park when it first opened in 1920 and the same park today.*
>
> *Summarise the information by selecting and reporting the main features, and make comparisons where relevant.*

Write at least 150 words.

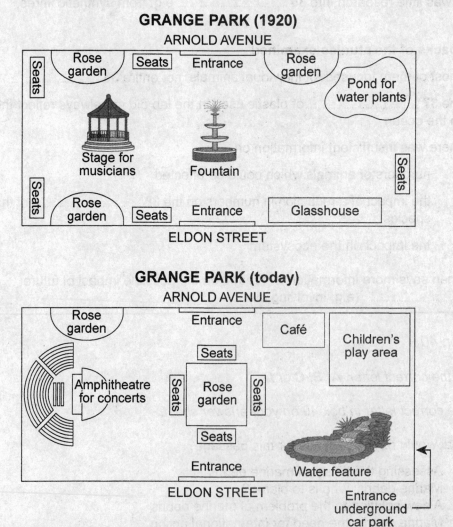

GRANGE PARK (1920)
ARNOLD AVENUE

Seats | Rose garden | Seats | Entrance | Rose garden | Pond for water plants

Stage for musicians

Fountain

Seats

Seats | Rose garden | Seats | Entrance | Glasshouse

ELDON STREET

GRANGE PARK (today)
ARNOLD AVENUE

Rose garden | Entrance | Café | Children's play area

Seats

Amphitheatre for concerts | Seats | Rose garden | Seats

Seats

Entrance | Water feature

ELDON STREET | Entrance underground car park

WRITING TASK 2

You should spend about 40 minutes on this task.

Write about the following topic:

> *Nowadays many people choose to be self-employed, rather than to work for a company or organisation.*
>
> *Why might this be the case?*
>
> *What could be the disadvantages of being self-employed?*

Give reasons for your answer and include any relevant examples from your own knowledge or experience.

Write at least 250 words.

SPEAKING

PART 1

The examiner asks the candidate about him/herself, his/her home, work or studies and other familiar topics.

EXAMPLE

Your neighbourhood

- Do you like the neighbourhood you live in? [Why/Why not?]
- What do you do in your neighbourhood in your free time? [Why/Why not?]
- What new things would you like to have in your neighbourhood? [Why/Why not?]
- Would you like to live in another neighbourhood in your town or city? [Why/Why not?]

PART 2

Describe a website you have bought something from.
You should say:
what the website is
what you bought from this website
how satisfied you were with what you bought
and explain what you liked and disliked about using this website.

You will have to talk about the topic for one to two minutes. You have one minute to think about what you are going to say. You can make some notes to help you if you wish.

PART 3

Discussion topics:

Shopping online

Example questions:
What kinds of things do people in your country often buy from online shops?
Why has online shopping become so popular in many countries?
What are some possible disadvantages of buying things from online shops?

Online retail businesses

Example questions:
Do you agree that the prices of all goods should be lower on internet shopping sites than in shops?
Will large shopping malls continue to be popular, despite the growth of internet shopping?
Do you think that some businesses (e.g. banks and travel agents) will only operate online in the future?

Audioscripts

TEST 1

SECTION 1

OFFICER:	Good morning. What can I do for you?
LOUISE:	I want to report a theft. I had some things stolen out of my bag yesterday.
OFFICER:	I'm sorry to hear that. Right, so I'll need to take a few details. Can I start with your name?
LOUISE:	Louise <u>Taylor</u>.
OFFICER:	OK, thank you. And are you resident in the UK?
LOUISE:	No, I'm actually <u>Canadian</u>, though my mother was British.
OFFICER:	And your date of birth?
LOUISE:	December 14th, 1977.
OFFICER:	So you're just visiting this country?
LOUISE:	That's right. I come over most summers on business. I'm an interior designer and I come over to buy old <u>furniture</u>, antiques you know. There are some really lovely things around here, but you need to get out to the small towns. I've had a really good trip this year, until this happened.
OFFICER:	OK. So you've been here quite a while?
LOUISE:	Yes, I'm here for two months. I go back next week.
OFFICER:	So may I ask where you're staying now?
LOUISE:	Well at present I've got a place at <u>Park</u> Apartments, that's on King Street. I was staying at the Riverside Apartments on the same street, but the apartment there was only available for six weeks so I had to find another one.
OFFICER:	OK. And the apartment number?
LOUISE:	Fifteen.
LOUISE:	Right.

Example

Q1

Q2

Q3

OFFICER:	Now, I need to take some details of the theft. So you said you had some things stolen out of your bag?
LOUISE:	That's right.
OFFICER:	And were you actually carrying the bag when the theft took place?
LOUISE:	Yes. I really can't understand it. I had my backpack on. And I went into a supermarket to buy a few things and when I opened it up my wallet wasn't there.
OFFICER:	And what did your wallet have in it?
LOUISE:	Well, fortunately I don't keep my credit cards in that wallet – I keep them with my passport in an inside compartment in my backpack. But there was quite a bit of cash there … about £<u>250</u> sterling, I should think. I withdrew £300 from my account yesterday, but I did a bit of shopping, so I must have already spent about £50 of that.
OFFICER:	OK.
LOUISE:	At first I thought, oh I must have left the wallet back in the apartment, but then I realised my <u>phone</u> had gone as well. It was only a week old, and that's when I realised I'd been robbed. Anyway at least they didn't take the keys to my rental car.

Q4

Q5

OFFICER:	Yes. So you say the theft occurred yesterday?	
LOUISE:	Yes.	
OFFICER:	So that was <u>September the tenth</u>. And do you have any idea at all of where or when the things might possibly have been stolen?	Q6
LOUISE:	Well at first I couldn't believe it because the bag had been on my back ever since I left the apartment after lunch. It's just a small backpack, but I generally use it when I'm travelling because it seems safer than a handbag. Anyway, I met up with a friend, and we spent a couple of hours in the <u>museum</u>. But I do remember that as we were leaving there, at about 4 o'clock, a group of young boys ran up to us, and they were really crowding round us, and they were asking us what <u>time</u> it was, then all of a sudden they ran off.	Q7 Q8
OFFICER:	Can you remember anything about them?	
LOUISE:	The one who did most of the talking was wearing a T-shirt with a picture of something ... let's see ... a tiger.	
OFFICER:	Right. Any idea of how old he might have been?	
LOUISE:	Around twelve years old?	
OFFICER:	And can you remember anything else about his appearance?	
LOUISE:	Not much. He was quite thin ...	
OFFICER:	Colour of hair?	
LOUISE:	I do remember that – he was <u>blond</u>. All the others were dark-haired.	Q9
OFFICER:	And any details of the others?	
LOUISE:	Not really. They came and went so quickly.	
OFFICER:	Right. So what I'm going to do now is give you a crime reference number so you can contact your insurance company. So this is ten digits: <u>87954 82361</u>.	Q10
LOUISE:	Thank you. So should I ...	

SECTION 2

Good morning everyone. My name's Janet Parker and I'm the human resources manager. We're very happy to welcome you to your new apprenticeship. I hope that the next six months will be a positive and enjoyable experience for you.

I'd like to start with some general advice about being an apprentice. Most of you have very little or no experience of working for a big organisation and the first week or so may be quite challenging. There will be a lot of new information to take in but don't worry too much about trying to remember everything. The important thing is to <u>check with someone if you're not sure what to do</u> – you'll find your supervisor is very approachable and won't mind explaining things or helping you out. You're here to learn so make the most of that opportunity. You'll be spending time in different departments during your first week so make an effort to <u>talk to as many people as possible</u> about their work – you'll make some new friends and find out lots of useful information.

Q11

Q12

As well as having a supervisor, you'll each be assigned a mentor. This person will be someone who's recently completed an apprenticeship and you'll meet with them on a weekly basis. Their role is to provide help and support throughout your apprenticeship. Of course, this doesn't mean they'll actually do any of your work for you – instead they'll be asking you about <u>what goals you've achieved so far</u>, as well as helping you to <u>identify any areas for improvement</u>. You can also <u>discuss your more long-term ambitions</u> with them as well.

Q13

Q14

Now I just want to run through a few company policies for our apprenticeship scheme with you... Most importantly, the internet. As part of your job you'll be doing some research online so obviously you'll have unlimited access for that but please <u>don't use it for personal use</u> – you'll have your own phones for that.

Q15

Some of you have already asked me about flexible working. After your probationary three-month period – some of you will be eligible for this – but <u>it will depend on which department you're in and what your personal circumstances are</u>. So please don't assume you'll automatically be permitted to do this.

Q16

I want to make sure there's no confusion about our holiday policy. Apart from any statutory public holidays <u>we ask that you don't book any holidays until after your six-month apprenticeship has finished</u>. Time off should only be taken if you are unwell. Please speak to your supervisor if this is going to be a problem.

Q17

You'll be expected to work a 40-hour week but there may be opportunities to do overtime during busy periods. Although you're not required to do this, <u>it can be a valuable experience – so we advise you to take it up if possible</u>. Obviously, we understand that people do have commitments outside work, so don't worry if there are times when you are unavailable.

Q18

As you know, we don't have a formal dress code here – you may wear casual clothes as long as they're practical – and the only restriction for shoes we have is on high heels for health and safety reasons. <u>Comfortable shoes like trainers are preferable</u>.

Q19

There's a heavily subsidised canteen on site where you can get hot meals or salads cheaply. Snacks and drinks are also provided – so <u>we've decided to introduce a no packed lunch policy</u>. This is partly to encourage healthy eating at work and partly to stop people from eating at their workstation, which is unhygienic.

Q20

OK moving on to …

SECTION 3

TUTOR:	OK, so what I'd like you to do now is to talk to your partner about your presentations on urban planning. You should have done most of the reading now, so I'd like you to share your ideas, and talk about the structure of your presentation and what you need to do next.
CARLA:	OK Rob. I'm glad we chose quite a specific topic – cities built next to the sea. It made it much easier to find relevant information.
ROB:	Yeah. And cities are growing so quickly – I mean, we know that more than half the world's population lives in cities now.
CARLA:	Yeah, though that's all cities, not just ones on the coast. But <u>most of the biggest cities are actually built by the sea</u>, I'd not realised that before.
ROB:	Nor me. And what's more, a lot of them are built at places where rivers come out into the sea. But apparently this can be a problem.
CARLA:	Why?
ROB:	Well, as the city expands, agriculture and industry tend to spread further inland along the rivers, and so agriculture moves even further inland up the river. That's not necessarily a problem, except <u>it means more and more pollutants are discharged into the rivers</u>.
CARLA:	So these are brought downstream to the cities?
ROB:	Right. Hmm. Did you read that article about Miami, on the east coast of the USA?
CARLA:	No.
ROB:	Well, apparently back in the 1950s they built channels to drain away the water in case of flooding.
CARLA:	Sounds sensible.
ROB:	Yeah, they spent quite a lot of money on them. <u>But what they didn't take into account was global warming</u>. So they built the drainage channels too close to sea level, and

Q21

Q22

Q23

now sea levels are rising, they're more or less useless. If there's a lot of rain, the water can't run away, there's nowhere for it to go. The whole design was faulty.

CARLA: So what are the authorities doing about it now?

ROB: I don't know. I did read that they're aiming to stop disposing of waste water into the ocean over the next ten years.

CARLA: But that won't help with flood prevention now, will it?

ROB: No. Really <u>they just need to find the money for something to replace the drainage channels</u>, in order to protect against flooding now. But in the long term they need to consider the whole ecosystem.   Q24

CARLA: Right. Really, though, coastal cities can't deal with their problems on their own, can they? I mean, they've got to start acting together at an international level instead of just doing their own thing.

ROB: Absolutely. The thing is, everyone knows what the problems are and environmentalists have a pretty good idea of what we should be doing about them, so <u>they should be able to work together</u> to some extent. But it's going to be a long time before countries come to a decision on what principles they're prepared to abide by.   Q25

CARLA: Yes, if they ever do.

CARLA: So I think we've probably got enough for our presentation. It's only fifteen minutes.

ROB: OK. So I suppose we'll begin with some general historical background about why coastal cities were established. But <u>we don't want to spend too long on that</u>, the other students will already know a bit about it. It's all to do with communications and so on.   Q26

CARLA: Yes. We should mention some geographical factors, things like wetlands and river estuaries and coastal erosion and so on. We could have some maps of different cities with these features marked.

ROB: On a handout you mean? Or <u>some slides everyone can see</u>?   Q27

CARLA: Yeah, that'd be better.

ROB: It'd be good to go into past mistakes in a bit more detail. Did you read that case study of the problems there were in New Orleans with flooding a few years ago?

CARLA: Yes. <u>We could use that as the basis for that part of the talk</u>. I don't think the other students will have read it, but they'll remember hearing about the flooding at the time.   Q28

ROB: OK. So that's probably enough background.

CARLA: So then we'll go on to talk about what action's being taken to deal with the problems of coastal cities.

ROB: OK. What else do we need to talk about? Maybe something on future risks, looking more at the long term, if populations continue to grow.

CARLA: Yeah. We'll need to do a bit of work there, I haven't got much information, have you?

ROB: No. <u>We'll need to look at some websites</u>. Shouldn't take too long.   Q29

CARLA: OK. And I think we should end by talking about international implications. Maybe <u>we could ask people in the audience</u>. We've got people from quite a lot of different places.   Q30

ROB: That'd be interesting, if we have time, yes. So now shall we …

SECTION 4

Producing enough energy to meet our needs has become a serious problem. Demand is rising rapidly, because of the world's increasing population and expanding <u>industry</u>. Burning fossil fuels, like gas, coal and oil, seriously damages the environment and they'll eventually run out. For a number of years now, scientists have been working out how we can derive energy from   Q31 renewable sources, such as the sun and wind, without causing pollution. Today I'll outline marine renewable energy – also called ocean energy – which harnesses the movement of the oceans.

Marine renewable energy can be divided into three main categories: wave energy, tidal energy and ocean thermal energy conversion, and I'll say a few words about each one.

First, wave energy. Numerous devices have been invented to harvest wave energy, with names such as Wave Dragon, the Penguin and Mighty Whale, and research is going on to try and come up with a really efficient method. This form of energy has plenty of potential, as the source is <u>constant</u>, and there's no danger of waves coming to a standstill. Electricity can be generated using onshore systems, using a reservoir, or offshore systems. But the problem with ocean waves is that they're erratic, with the wind making them travel in every <u>direction</u>. This adds to the difficulty of creating efficient technology: ideally all the waves would travel smoothly and regularly along the same straight line. Another drawback is that sand and other sediment on the ocean <u>floor</u> might be stopped from flowing normally, which can lead to environmental problems.   *Q32* *Q33* *Q34*

The second category of marine energy that I'll mention is tidal energy. One major advantage of using the tide, rather than waves, as a source of energy is that it's <u>predictable</u>: we know the exact times of high and low tides for years to come.   *Q35*

For tidal energy to be effective, the difference between high and low tides needs to be at least five metres, and this occurs naturally in only about forty places on Earth. But the right conditions can be created by constructing a tidal lagoon, an area of sea water separated from the sea.

One current plan is to create a tidal lagoon on the coast of Wales. This will be an area of water within a <u>bay</u> at Swansea, sheltered by a U-shaped breakwater, or dam, built out from the coast. The breakwater will contain sixteen hydro turbines, and as the tide rises, water rushes through the breakwater, activating the turbines, which turn a generator to produce electricity. Then, for three hours as the tide goes out, the water is held back within the breakwater, increasing the difference in water level, until it's several metres higher within the lagoon than in the open sea. Then, in order to release the stored water, <u>gates</u> in the breakwater are opened. It pours powerfully out of the lagoon, driving the turbines in the breakwater in the opposite direction and again generating thousands of megawatts of electricity. As there are two high tides a day, this lagoon scheme would generate electricity four times a day, every day, for a total of around 14 hours in every 24 – and enough electricity for over 150,000 homes.   *Q36* *Q37*

This system has quite a lot in its favour: unlike solar and wind energy it doesn't depend on the weather; the turbines are operated without the need for <u>fuel</u>, so it doesn't create any greenhouse gas emissions; and very little maintenance is needed. It's estimated that electricity generated in this way will be relatively cheap, and that manufacturing the components would create more than 2,000 <u>jobs</u>, a big boost to the local economy.   *Q38* *Q39*

On the other hand, there are fears that lagoons might harm both fish and birds, for example by disturbing <u>migration</u> patterns, and causing a build-up of silt, affecting local ecosystems.   *Q40*

There are other forms of tidal energy, but I'll go on to the third category of marine energy: ocean thermal energy conversion. This depends on there being a big difference in temperature between surface water and the water a couple of kilometres below the surface, and this occurs in tropical coastal areas. The idea is to bring cold water up to the surface using a submerged pipe. The concept dates back to 1881, when ...

TEST 2

SECTION 1

CARL: Hi, come and take a seat.

JULIE: Thank you.

CARL: My name's Carl Rogers and I'm one of the doctors here at the Total Health Clinic. So I understand this is your first visit to the clinic?

JULIE: Yes, it is.

CARL: OK, well I hope you'll be very happy with the service you receive here. So if it's alright with you I'll take a few details to help me give you the best possible service.

JULIE: Sure.

CARL: So can I check first of all that we have the correct personal details for you? So your full name is Julie Anne Garcia? *Example*

JULIE: That's correct.

CARL: Perfect. And can I have a contact phone number? *Q1*

JULIE: It's 219 442 9785.

CARL: OK, and then can I just check that we have the correct date of birth?

JULIE: October tenth, 1992. *Q2*

CARL: Oh, I actually have 1991, I'll just correct that now. Right, so that's all good. Now I just need just a few more personal details ... do you have an occupation, either full-time or part-time?

JULIE: Yes, I work full-time in Esterhazy's – you know, the restaurant chain. I started off as a waitress there a few years ago and I'm a manager now. *Q3*

CARL: Oh I know them, yeah, they're down on 114th Street, aren't they?

JULIE: That's right.

CARL: Yeah, I've been there a few times. I just love their salads.

JULIE: That's good to hear.

CARL: Right, so one more thing I need to know before we talk about why you're here, Julie, and that's the name of your insurance company.

JULIE: It's Cawley Life Insurance, that's C-A-W-L-E-Y. *Q4*

CARL: Excellent, thank you so much.

CARL: Now Julie, let's look at how we can help you. So tell me a little about what brought you here today.

JULIE: Well, I've been getting a pain in my knee, the left one. Not very serious at first, but it's gotten worse, so I thought I ought to see someone about it. *Q5*

CARL: That's certainly the right decision. So how long have you been aware of this pain? Is it just a few days, or is it longer than that?

JULIE: Longer. It's been worse for the last couple of days, but it's three weeks since I first noticed it. It came on quite gradually though, so I kind of ignored it at first. *Q6*

CARL: And have you taken any medication yourself, or treated it in anyway?

JULIE: Yeah, I've been taking medication to deal with the pain, Tylenol, and that works OK for a few hours. But I don't like to keep taking it.

CARL: OK. And what about heat treatment? Have you tried applying heat at all?

JULIE: No, but I have been using ice on it for the last few days.

CARL: And does that seem to help the pain at all?

JULIE: A little, yes.

CARL: Good. Now you look as if you're quite fit normally?

JULIE:	I am, yes.	
CARL:	So do you do any sport on a regular basis?	
JULIE:	Yes, I play a lot of <u>tennis</u>. I belong to a club so I go there a lot. I'm quite competitive so I enjoy that side of it as well as the exercise. But I haven't gone since this started.	Q7
CARL:	Sure. And do you do any other types of exercise?	
JULIE:	Yeah, I sometimes do a little swimming, but usually just when I'm on vacation. But normally I go <u>running</u> a few times a week, maybe three or four times.	Q8
CARL:	Hmm. So your legs are getting quite a pounding. But you haven't had any problems up to now?	
JULIE:	No, not with my legs. I did have an accident last year when I slipped and hurt my <u>shoulder</u>, but that's better now.	Q9
CARL:	Excellent. And do you have any allergies?	
JULIE:	No, none that I'm aware of.	
CARL:	And do you take any medication on a regular basis?	
JULIE:	Well, I take <u>vitamins</u> but that's all. I'm generally very healthy.	Q10
CARL:	OK, well let's have a closer look and see what might be causing this problem. If you can just get up …	

SECTION 2

We'll be arriving at Branley Castle in about five minutes, but before we get there I'll give you a little information about the castle and what our visit will include.

So in fact there's been a castle on this site for over eleven hundred years. The first building was a fort constructed in 914 AD for defence against Danish invaders by King Alfred the Great's daughter, who ruled England at the time. In the following century, after the Normans conquered England, the land was given to a nobleman called Richard de Vere, and he built a castle there that stayed in the de Vere family for over four hundred years.

However, when Queen Elizabeth I announced that she was going to visit the castle in 1576 it was beginning to look a bit run down, and it was decided that rather than repair the guest rooms, <u>they'd make a new house for her</u> out of wood next to the main hall. She stayed there for four nights and apparently it was very luxurious, but unfortunately it was destroyed a few years later by fire.   Q11

In the seventeenth century the castle belonged to the wealthy Fenys family, who enlarged it and made it more comfortable. However, by 1982 the Fenys family could no longer afford to maintain the castle, even though they received government support, and they put it on the market. It was eventually taken over by <u>a company who owned a number of amusement parks</u>, but when we get there I think you'll see that they've managed to retain the original atmosphere of the castle.   Q12

When you go inside, you'll find that in the state rooms <u>there are life-like moving wax models dressed in costumes of different periods in the past</u>, which even carry on conversations together. As well as that, in every room there are booklets giving information about what the room was used for and the history of the objects and furniture it contains.   Q13

The castle park's quite extensive. At one time sheep were kept there, and in the nineteenth century the owners had a little zoo with animals like rabbits and even a baby elephant. Nowadays the old zoo buildings are used for <u>public displays of paintings and sculpture</u>. The park also has some beautiful trees, though the oldest of all, which dated back 800 years, was sadly blown down in 1987.   Q14

Now, you're free to wander around on your own until 4.30, but then at the end of our visit we'll all meet together at the bottom of the Great Staircase. We'll then go on to the long gallery, where there's a wonderful collection of photographs showing the family who owned the castle a hundred years ago having tea and cakes in the conservatory – and we'll then take you to <u>the same place, where afternoon tea will be served</u> to you.　　　　　*Q15*

Now if you can take a look at your plans you'll see Branley Castle has four towers, joined together by a high wall, with the river on two sides.

Don't miss seeing the Great Hall. That's near the river in the main tower, the biggest one, which was extended and redesigned in the eighteenth century.

If you want to get a good view of the whole castle, you can walk around the walls. <u>The</u>　*Q16*
<u>starting point's quite near the main entrance – walk straight down the path until you get to the</u>
<u>south gate, and it's just there</u>. Don't go on to the north gate – there's no way up from there.

There'll shortly be a show in which you can see archers displaying their skill with a bow and arrow. The quickest way to get there is to <u>take the first left after the main entrance and follow</u>　*Q17*
<u>the path past the bridge, then you'll see it in front of you at the end</u>.

If you like animals there's also a display of hunting birds – falcons and eagles and so on. If you <u>go from the main entrance in the direction of the south gate, but turn right before you get</u>　*Q18*
<u>there instead of going through it, you'll see it on your right past the first tower</u>.

At 3 pm there's a short performance of traditional dancing on the <u>outdoor stage. That's right</u>　*Q19*
<u>at the other side of the castle from the entrance, and over the bridge</u>. It's about ten minutes' walk or so.

And finally the shop. It's actually <u>inside one of the towers, but the way in is from the outside.</u>　*Q20*
<u>Just take the first left after the main entrance, go down the path and take the first right</u>. It's got some lovely gifts and souvenirs.

Right, so we're just arriving …

SECTION 3

TUTOR:	So, Rosie and Martin, let's look at what you've got for your presentation on woolly mammoths.
ROSIE:	OK, we've got a short outline here.
TUTOR:	Thanks. So it's about a research project in North America?
MARTIN:	Yes. But we thought we needed something general about woolly mammoths in our introduction, to establish that they were related to our modern elephant, and they lived thousands of years ago in the last ice age.
ROSIE:	Maybe we could show a video clip of a cartoon about mammoths. But that'd be a bit childish. Or we could have a diagram, <u>it could be a timeline to show when they</u> *Q21* <u>lived, with illustrations</u>?
MARTIN:	Or we could just show a drawing of them walking in the ice? No, let's go with your last suggestion.
TUTOR:	Good. Then you're describing the discovery of the mammoth tooth on St Paul's Island in Alaska, and why it was significant.

ROSIE: Yes. The tooth was found by a man called Russell Graham. He picked it up from under a rock in a cave. He knew it was special – for a start it was in really good condition, as if it had been just extracted from the animal's jawbone. Anyway, they found it was 6,500 years old.

TUTOR: So why was that significant?

ROSIE: Well the mammoth bones previously found on the North American mainland were much less recent than that. So this was really amazing.   Q22

MARTIN: Then we're making an animated diagram to show the geography of the area in prehistoric times. So originally, St Paul's Island wasn't an island, it was connected to the mainland, and mammoths and other animals like bears were able to roam around the whole area.

ROSIE: Then the climate warmed up and the sea level began to rise, and the island got cut off from the mainland. So those mammoths on the island couldn't escape; they had to stay on the island.   Q23

MARTIN: And in fact the species survived there for thousands of years after they'd become extinct on the mainland.

TUTOR: So why do you think they died out on the mainland?

ROSIE: No one's sure.

MARTIN: Anyway, next we'll explain how Graham and his team identified the date when the mammoths became extinct on the *island*. They concluded that the extinction happened 5,600 years ago, which is a very precise time for a prehistoric extinction. It's based on samples they took from mud at the bottom of a lake on the island. They analysed it to find out what had fallen in over time – bits of plants, volcanic ash and even DNA from the mammoths themselves. It's standard procedure, but it took nearly two years to do.   Q24

TUTOR: So why don't you quickly go through the main sections of your presentation and discuss what action's needed for each part?

MARTIN: OK. So for the introduction, we're using a visual, so once we've prepared that we're done.

ROSIE: I'm not sure. I think we need to write down all the ideas we want to include here, not just rely on memory. How we begin the presentation is so important ...   Q25

MARTIN: You're right.

ROSIE: The discovery of the mammoth tooth is probably the most dramatic part, but we don't have that much information, only what we got from the online article. I thought maybe we could get in touch with the researcher who led the team and ask him to tell us a bit more.   Q26

MARTIN: Great idea. What about the section with the initial questions asked by the researchers? We've got a lot on that but we need to make it interesting.

ROSIE: We could ask the audience to suggest some questions about it and then see how many of them we can answer. I don't think it would take too long.   Q27

TUTOR: Yes that would add a bit of variety.

MARTIN: Then the section on further research carried out on the island – analysing the mud in the lake. I wonder if we've actually got too much information here, should we cut some?

ROSIE: I don't think so, but it's all a bit muddled at present.

MARTIN: Yes, maybe it would be better if it followed a chronological pattern.   Q28

ROSIE: I think so. The findings and possible explanations section is just about ready, but we need to practise it so we're sure it won't overrun.   Q29

MARTIN: I think it should be OK, but yes, let's make sure.

TUTOR: In the last section, relevance to the present day, you've got some good ideas but this is where you need to move away from the ideas of others and <u>give your own</u>   *Q30*
<u>viewpoint</u>.

MARTIN: OK, we'll think about that. Now shall we ...

SECTION 4

In this series of lectures about the history of weather forecasting, I'll start by examining its early history – that'll be the subject of today's talk.

OK, so we'll start by going back thousands of years. Most ancient cultures had weather gods, and weather catastrophes, such as floods, played an important role in many creation myths. Generally, weather was attributed to the whims of the gods, as the wide range of weather gods in various cultures shows. For instance, there's the Egyptian sun god Ra, and Thor, the Norse god of thunder and lightning. Many ancient civilisations developed rites such as <u>dances</u> in order to make the weather gods look kindly on them.   *Q31*

But the weather was of daily importance: observing the skies and drawing the correct conclusions from these observations was really important, in fact their <u>survival</u> depended on   *Q32*
it. It isn't known when people first started to observe the skies, but at around 650 BC, the Babylonians produced the first short-range weather forecasts, based on their observations of <u>clouds</u> and other phenomena. The Chinese also recognised weather patterns, and by   *Q33*
300 BC, astronomers had developed a calendar which divided the year into 24 <u>festivals</u>,   *Q34*
each associated with a different weather phenomenon.

The ancient Greeks were the first to develop a more scientific approach to explaining the weather. The work of the philosopher and scientist Aristotle, in the fourth century BC, is especially noteworthy, as his ideas held sway for nearly 2,000 years. In 340 BC, he wrote a book in which he attempted to account for the formation of rain, clouds, wind and storms. He also described celestial phenomena such as haloes – that is, bright circles of light around the sun, the moon and bright stars – and <u>comets</u>. Many of his observations were surprisingly   *Q35*
accurate. For example, he believed that heat could cause water to evaporate. But he also jumped to quite a few wrong conclusions, such as that winds are breathed out by the Earth. Errors like this were rectified from the Renaissance onwards.

For nearly 2,000 years, Aristotle's work was accepted as the chief authority on weather theory. Alongside this, though, in the Middle Ages weather observations were passed on in the form of proverbs, such as 'Red <u>sky</u> at night, shepherd's delight; red sky in the morning,   *Q36*
shepherd's warning'. Many of these are based on very good observations and are accurate, as contemporary meteorologists have discovered.

For centuries, any attempt to forecast the weather could only be based on personal observations, but in the fifteenth century scientists began to see the need for <u>instruments</u>.   *Q37*
Until then, the only ones available were weather vanes – to determine the wind direction – and early versions of rain gauges. One of the first, invented in the fifteenth century, was a hygrometer, which measured humidity. This was one of many inventions that contributed to the development of weather forecasting.

In 1592, the Italian scientist and inventor Galileo developed the world's first <u>thermometer</u>. His   *Q38*
student Torricelli later invented the barometer, which allowed people to measure atmospheric pressure. In 1648, the French philosopher Pascal proved that pressure decreases with altitude. This discovery was verified by English astronomer Halley in 1686; and Halley was also the first person to map trade winds.

This increasing ability to measure factors related to weather helped scientists to understand the atmosphere and its processes better, and they started collecting weather observation data systematically. In the eighteenth century, the scientist and politician Benjamin Franklin carried out work on electricity and lightning in particular, but he was also very interested in weather and studied it throughout most of his life. It was Franklin who discovered that <u>storms</u>   *Q39* generally travel from west to east.

In addition to new meteorological instruments, other developments contributed to our understanding of the atmosphere. People in different locations began to keep records, and in the mid-nineteenth century, the invention of the <u>telegraph</u> made it possible for these records   *Q40* to be collated. This led, by the end of the nineteenth century, to the first weather services.

It was not until the early twentieth century that mathematics and physics became part of meteorology, and we'll continue from that point next week.

SECTION 1

ANGELA:	Hello, Flanders conference hotel.
MAN:	Oh, hi. I wanted to ask about conference facilities at the hotel. Have I come through to the right person?
ANGELA:	You have. I'm the customer services manager. My name's <u>Angela</u>. So how can I help you?

Example

MAN:	Well, I'm calling from Barrett and Stansons, we're a medical company based in Perth.
ANGELA:	Oh yes.
MAN:	And we're organising a conference for our clients to be held in Sydney. It'll be held over two days and we're expecting about fifty or sixty people.
ANGELA:	When were you thinking of having it?
MAN:	Some time early next year, like the end of January? It'd have to be a weekend.
ANGELA:	Let me see … our conference facilities are already booked for the weekend beginning January 28th. We could do the first weekend in February?
MAN:	How about January 21st?
ANGELA:	I'm afraid that's booked too.
MAN:	Well, let's go for the February date then.
ANGELA:	So that's the weekend beginning the 4th.
MAN:	OK. Now can you tell me a bit about what conference facilities you have?
ANGELA:	Sure. So for talks and presentations we have the Tesla room.
MAN:	Sorry?
ANGELA:	<u>Tesla</u> – that's spelled T-E-S-L-A. It holds up to a hundred people, and it's fully equipped with a projector and so on.
MAN:	How about a <u>microphone</u>?
ANGELA:	Yes, that'll be all set up ready for you, and there'll be one that members of the audience can use too, for questions, if necessary.
MAN:	Fine. And we'll also need some sort of open area where people can sit and have a cup of coffee, and we'd like to have an <u>exhibition</u> of our products and services there as well, so that'll need to be quite a big space.
ANGELA:	That's fine, there's a central atrium with all those facilities, and you can come before the conference starts if you want to set everything up.
MAN:	Great. And I presume there's <u>wifi</u>?
ANGELA:	Oh yes, that's free and available throughout the hotel.
MAN:	OK.
ANGELA:	Would you also like us to provide a buffet lunch? We can do a two-course meal with a number of different options.
MAN:	What sort of price are we looking at for that?
ANGELA:	Well, I can send you a copy of the standard menu. That's $<u>45</u> per person. Or you can have the special for $25 more.
MAN:	I think the standard should be OK, but yes, send me the menu.

Q1

Q2

Q3

Q4

Q5

MAN:	Now we're also going to need accommodation on the Saturday night for some of the participants … I'm not sure how many, but probably about 25. So what do you charge for a room?
ANGELA:	Well, for conference attendees we have a 25% reduction, so we can offer you rooms at $<u>135</u>. Normally a standard room's $180.

Q6

MAN:	And does that include breakfast?	
ANGELA:	Sure. And of course, guests can also make use of all the other facilities at the hotel. So we've got a spa where you can get massages and facials and so on, and there's a <u>pool</u> up on the roof for the use of guests.	Q7
MAN:	Great. Now what about transport links? The hotel's downtown, isn't it?	
ANGELA:	Yes, it's about 12 kilometres from the <u>airport</u>, but there's a complimentary shuttle bus for guests. And it's only about ten minutes' walk from the central railway station.	Q8
MAN:	OK. Now, I don't know Sydney very well, can you just give me an idea of the location of the hotel?	
ANGELA:	Well, it's downtown on Wilby Street, that's quite a small street, and it's not very far from the <u>sea</u>. And of course if the conference attendees want to go out on the Saturday evening there's a huge choice of places to eat. Then if they want to make a night of it, they can go on to one of the <u>clubs</u> in the area – there are a great many to choose from.	Q9 Q10
MAN:	OK. So if we go ahead with this, can you give me some information about how much …	

SECTION 2

Good morning. My name's Lucy Crittenden, and I'm the Director of Operations for an organisation that arranges volunteering in this part of the country. I'm hoping I can persuade one or two of you to become volunteers yourselves. Let me start by briefly explaining what we mean by volunteering.

Volunteers are teenagers and adults who choose to spend some time, unpaid, helping other people in some way. Most volunteers devote two or three hours to this every week, while a few do much more. The people they help may have physical or behavioural difficulties, for example.

Volunteers can do all sorts of things, depending on their own abilities and interests. If they're supporting a family that's struggling, for example, they may be able to give them tips on cooking, or recommend how to plan their budget or how to shop sensibly on their income. They might even do <u>some painting or wallpapering</u>, perhaps alongside any members of the Q11
family who are able to do it. Or even do <u>some babysitting</u> so that parents can go out for Q12
a while.

The benefit from volunteering isn't only for the people being helped. Volunteers also gain from it: they're using their skills to cope with somebody's mental or physical ill health, and <u>volunteering may be a valuable element of their CV when they're applying for jobs</u>: employers Q13
usually look favourably on someone who's given up time to help others. Significantly, most volunteers <u>feel that what they're doing gives them a purpose in their lives</u>. And in my opinion, Q14
they're lucky in that respect, as many people don't have that feeling.

Now I'd like to tell you what some of our volunteers have said about what they do, to give you an idea of the range of ways in which they can help people.

Habib supports an elderly lady who's beginning to show signs of dementia. Once a week they, along with other elderly people, go to the local community centre, where a group of people come in and sing. The songs <u>take the listeners back to their youth</u>, and for a little Q15
while they can forget the difficulties that they face now.

Our volunteer Consuela is an amazing woman. <u>She has difficulty walking herself, but she doesn't let that stop her</u>. She helps a couple of people with similar difficulties, who had almost stopped walking altogether. <u>By using herself as an example, Consuela encourages them to walk more and more</u>. **Q16**

Minh visits a young man who lives alone and can't leave his home on his own, so he hardly ever saw anyone. But together <u>they go out to the cinema, or to see friends</u> the young man hadn't been able to visit for a long time. **Q17**

Tanya visits an elderly woman once a week. When the woman found out that Tanya is a professional dressmaker, she got interested. Tanya showed her some soft toys she'd made, and <u>the woman decided to try it herself</u>. And now she really enjoys it, and spends hours making toys. They're not perhaps up to Tanya's standard yet, but she gains a lot of pleasure from doing it. **Q18**

Alexei is a volunteer with a family that faces a number of difficulties. By calmly talking over possible solutions with family members, he's helping them to realise that they aren't helpless, and that <u>they can do something themselves to improve their situation</u>. This has been great for their self-esteem. **Q19**

And the last volunteer I'll mention, though there are plenty more, is Juba. She volunteers with a teenage girl with learning difficulties, who wasn't very good at talking to other people. Juba's worked very patiently with her, <u>and now the girl is far better at expressing herself, and at understanding other people</u>. **Q20**

OK, I hope that's given you an idea of what volunteering is all about. Now I'd like …

SECTION 3

LIZZIE:	So how are you getting on with your teaching practice at the High School, Joe?
JOE:	Well I've been put in charge of the school marching band, and it's quite a responsibility. I'd like to talk it over with you.
LIZZIE:	Go ahead. You'd better start by giving me a bit of background.
JOE:	OK. Well the band has students in it from all years, so they're aged 11 to 18, and there are about <u>50</u> of them altogether. It's quite a popular activity within the school. I've never worked with a band of more than 20 before, and this is very different. **Q21**
LIZZIE:	I can imagine.
JOE:	They aren't really good enough to enter national band competitions, but they're in a <u>regional</u> one later in the term. Even if they don't win, and I don't expect them to, hopefully it'll be an incentive for them to try and improve. **Q22**
LIZZIE:	Yes, hopefully.
JOE:	Well, now the town council's organising a <u>carnival</u> in the summer, and the band has been asked to perform. If you ask me, they aren't really up to it yet, and I need to get them functioning better as a band, and in a very short time. **Q23**
LIZZIE:	Have you been doing anything with them? Apart from practising the music, I mean.
JOE:	I played a recording I came across, of a <u>drummer</u> talking about how playing in a band had changed his life. I think it was an after-dinner speech. I thought it was pretty inspiring, because being in the band had stopped him from getting involved in crime. The students seemed to find it interesting, too. **Q24**

LIZZIE:	That's good.	
JOE:	I'm planning to show them that old <u>film</u> from the 1940s 'Strike Up the Band', and talk about it with the students. What do you think?	Q25
LIZZIE:	Good idea. As it's about a school band, it might make the students realise how much they can achieve if they work together.	
JOE:	That's what I've got in mind. I'm hoping I can take some of the band to a <u>parade</u> that's going to take place next month. A couple of marching bands will be performing, and the atmosphere should be quite exciting. It depends on whether I can persuade the school to hire a coach or two to take us there.	Q26
LIZZIE:	Mmm. They sound like good ideas to me.	
JOE:	Thanks.	

JOE:	Can I tell you about a few people in the band who I'm finding it quite difficult to cope with? I'm sure you'll have some ideas about what I can do.	
LIZZIE:	Go ahead.	
JOE:	There's a flautist who says she loves playing in the band. We rehearse twice a week after school, but <u>she's hardly ever there</u>. Then she looks for me the next day and gives me a very plausible reason – she says she had to help her mother, or she's been ill, but to be honest, I don't believe her.	Q27
LIZZIE:	Oh dear! Any more students with difficulties?	
JOE:	Plenty! There's a trumpeter who thinks she's the best musician in the band, though she certainly isn't. <u>She's always saying what she thinks other people should do</u>, which makes my job pretty difficult.	Q28
LIZZIE:	She sounds a bit of a nightmare!	
JOE:	You can say that again. One of the trombonists has got an impressive sense of rhythm, and could be an excellent musician – except that <u>he has breathing difficulties, and he doesn't really have enough breath for the trombone</u>. He'd be much better off playing percussion, for instance, but he refuses to give up. So he ends up only playing half the notes.	Q29
LIZZIE:	I suppose you have to admire his determination.	
JOE:	Maybe. One of the percussionists isn't too bad, but <u>he never seems to interact with other people, and he always rushes off as soon as the rehearsal ends</u>. I don't know if there are family reasons, or what. But it isn't good in a band, where people really need to feel they're part of a group.	Q30
LIZZIE:	Hmm.	
JOE:	There are others too, but at least that gives you an idea of what I'm up against. Do you have any thoughts about what I can do, Lizzie?	

SECTION 4

As you all know, the university is planning an arts festival for later this year, and here in the music department we've planned three concerts. These will be public performances, and the programme has just been finalised. The theme of the festival is links between the UK and Australia, and this is reflected in the music: each concert will feature both British and Australian composers. I'll tell you briefly about the Australian music, as you probably won't be familiar with that.

Audioscripts

The first concert will include music by Liza Lim, who was born in Perth, Western Australia, in 1966. As a child, Lim originally learned to play the piano – like so many children – and also the <u>violin</u>, but when she was 11 her teachers encouraged her to start composing. She found   *Q31* this was her real strength, and she studied and later taught composition, both in Australia and in other countries. As a composer, she has received commissions from numerous orchestras, other performers and festivals in several countries.

Liza Lim's compositions are vibrant and full of <u>energy</u>, and she often explores Asian and   *Q32* Australian Aboriginal cultural sources, including the native instrument, the didgeridoo: this is featured in a work called *The Compass.* Her music is very expressive, so although it is <u>complex</u>, it has the power of connecting with audiences and performers alike.   *Q33*

In the festival we're going to give a semi-staged performance of *The Oresteia.* This is an <u>opera</u> in seven parts, based on the trilogy of ancient Greek tragedies by Aeschylus. Lim   *Q34* composed this when she was in her mid-20s, and she also wrote the text, along with Barrie Kosky. It's performed by six singers, a dancer, and an orchestra that, as well as standard orchestral instruments, includes electric guitar, and a traditional Turkish stringed instrument. Lim wrote that because the stories in the tragedies are not easy to tell, the sounds she creates are also <u>disturbing</u>, and they include breathing, sobbing, laughing and whistling. The   *Q35* work lasts around 75 minutes, and the rest of the concert will consist of orchestral works by the British composers Ralph Vaughan Williams and Frederick Delius.

Moving on now to our second concert, this will begin with instrumental music by British composers – Benjamin Britten and Judith Weir. After the interval we'll go to Australia for a piece by Ross Edwards: *The Tower of Remoteness.* According to Edwards, the inspiration for this piece came from nature, when he was sitting alone in the dry bed of a creek, overshadowed by the leaves of palm trees, listening to the birds and insects. *The Tower of Remoteness* is scored for piano and <u>clarinet</u>. Edwards says he realised years after writing the   *Q36* piece that he had subconsciously modelled its opening phrase on a bird call.

Ross Edwards was born in 1943 in Sydney, Australia, and studied at the Sydney Conservatorium of Music and the universities of Adelaide and Sydney. He's well known in Australia, and in fact he's one of the country's most performed composers. He's written a wide range of music, from symphonies and concertos to some composed specifically for children. Edwards's music has been described as being 'deeply connected to Australia', and it can be regarded as a celebration of the <u>diversity</u> of cultures that Australia can be proud of.   *Q37*

The last of the three Australian composers to be represented in our festival is Carl Vine. Born in 1954, Vine, like Liza Lim, comes from Perth, Western Australia. He took up the cornet at the age of five, switching to the piano five years later. However, he went to university to study <u>physics</u>, before changing to composition. After graduating he moved to Sydney and worked   *Q38* as a freelance pianist and composer. Before long he had become prominent in Australia as a composer for <u>dance</u>, and in fact has written 25 scores of that type.   *Q39*

In our third concert, Vine will be represented by his music for the flag hand-over ceremony of the <u>Olympics</u> held in 1996. This seven-minute orchestral piece was of course heard by   *Q40* millions of people worldwide, and we'll hear it alongside works written by British composers Edward Elgar and, more recently, Thomas Adès.

TEST 4

SECTION 1

ANDREW:	Good morning, Clare House Hotel. Andrew speaking. I'm the <u>Events</u> Manager.	*Example*
SAM:	Good morning, Andrew. My name's Samantha. I'm arranging a party for my parents' fiftieth wedding anniversary, and I'm ringing to ask about hiring a room some time next September. Also my parents and several of the guests will need accommodation.	
ANDREW:	OK, I'm sure we can help you with that. Will you be having a sit-down meal or a buffet?	
SAM:	Probably a sit-down.	
ANDREW:	And do you know how many people there'll be?	
SAM:	Around eighty, I think.	
ANDREW:	Well we have two rooms that can hold that number. One is the Adelphi Room. That can seat <u>eighty-five</u>, or hold over a hundred if people are standing for a buffet.	*Q1*
SAM:	Right.	
ANDREW:	If you have live music, there's room for four or five musicians in the gallery overlooking the room. Our guests usually appreciate the fact that the music can be loud enough for dancing, but not too loud for conversation.	
SAM:	Yes, I really don't like it when you can't talk.	
ANDREW:	Exactly. Now the Adelphi Room is at the back of the hotel, and there are French windows leading out onto the terrace. This has a beautiful display of pots of <u>roses</u> at that time of the year.	*Q2*
SAM:	Which direction does it face?	
ANDREW:	Southwest, so that side of the hotel gets the sun in the afternoon and early evening.	
SAM:	Very nice.	
ANDREW:	From the terrace you can see the area of <u>trees</u> within the grounds of the hotel, or you can stroll through there to the river – that's on the far side, so it isn't visible from the hotel.	*Q3*
SAM:	OK.	
ANDREW:	Then another option is the Carlton Room. This is a bit bigger – it can hold up to a hundred and ten people – and it has the advantage of a <u>stage</u>, which is useful if you have any entertainment, or indeed a small band can fit onto it.	*Q4*
SAM:	And can you go outside from the room?	
ANDREW:	No, the Carlton Room is on the first floor, but on one side the windows look out onto the lake.	
SAM:	Lovely. I think either of those rooms would be suitable.	
ANDREW:	Can I tell you about some of the options we offer in addition?	
SAM:	Please do.	
ANDREW:	As well as a meal, you can have an MC, a Master of Ceremonies, who'll be with you throughout the party.	
SAM:	What exactly is the MC's function? I suppose they make a <u>speech</u> during the meal if we need one, do they?	*Q5*
ANDREW:	That's right. All our MCs are trained as public speakers, so they can easily get people's attention – many guests are glad to have someone who can make themselves heard above the chatter! And they're also your <u>support</u> – if anything goes wrong, the MC will deal with it, so you can relax.	*Q6*

SAM:	Great! I'll need to ask you about food, but something else that's important is accommodation. You obviously have rooms in the hotel, but do you also have any other accommodation, like <u>cabins</u>, for example?	Q7
ANDREW:	Yes, there are five in the grounds, all self-contained. They each sleep two to four people and have their own living room, bathroom and small kitchen.	
SAM:	That sounds perfect for what we'll need.	

SAM:	Now you have various facilities, don't you? Are they all included in the price of hiring the room? The pool, for instance.	
ANDREW:	Normally you'd be able to use it, but <u>it'll be closed throughout September for refurbishment</u>, I'm afraid. <u>The gym will be available, though, at no extra charge</u>. That's open all day, from six in the morning until midnight.	Q8 Q9
SAM:	Right.	
ANDREW:	And the tennis courts, but <u>there is a small additional payment for those</u>. We have four courts, and it's worth booking in advance if you possibly can, as there can be quite a long waiting list for them!	Q10
SAM:	Right. Now could we discuss the food? This would be dinner, around seven o'clock ...	

SECTION 2

Hello everyone. I'm Jake Stevens and I'm your rep here at the hotel. I'm sure you'll all have a great time here. So let me tell you a bit about what's on offer. I'll start by telling you about some of the excursions that are available for guests.

One thing you have to do while you're here is go dolphin watching. On our boat trips, we pretty well guarantee you'll see dolphins – if you don't you can repeat the trip free of charge. We organise daily trips for just 35 euros. Unfortunately <u>there aren't any places left for this afternoon's trip</u>, but come and see me to book for later in the week. **Q11**

If you're energetic, I'd recommend our forest walk. It's a guided walk of about seven kilometres. There'll be a stop half way, and <u>you'll be provided with a drink and sandwiches</u>. There's some fairly steep climbs up the hills, so you need to be reasonably fit for this one, with good shoes, and bring a waterproof in case it rains. It's just 25 euros all inclusive, and it's every Wednesday. **Q12**

Then on Thursdays we organise a cycle trip, which will give you all the fun of biking without the effort. We'll take you and your bike up to the top of Mount Larna, and leave you to bike back – <u>it's a 700-metre drop in just 20 kilometres</u> so this isn't really for inexperienced cyclists as you'll be going pretty fast. And if it's a clear day, you'll have fantastic views. **Q13**

On our local craft tour you can find out about the traditional activities in the island. And the best thing about this trip is that <u>it's completely free</u>. You'll be taken to a factory where jewellery is made, and also a ceramics centre. If you want, you can buy some of the products but that's entirely up to you. The trip starts after lunch on Thursday, and you'll return by 6 pm. **Q14**

If you're interested in astronomy you may already know that the island's one of the best places in the world to observe the night sky. We can offer trips to the observatory on Friday for those who are interested. They cost 90 euros per person and you'll be shown the huge telescopes and have a talk from an expert, who'll explain all about how they work. <u>Afterwards we'll head down to Sunset Beach, where you can have a dip in the ocean</u> if you want before we head off back to the hotel. **Q15**

Finally, there's horse riding. This is organised by the Equestrian Centre over near Playa Cortino and it's a great experience if you're a keen horseback rider, <u>or even if you've never been on a horse before</u>. They take you down to the beach, and you can canter along the sand and through the waves. It costs 35 euros and it's available every day.

Q16

So there's plenty to do in the daytime, but what about night life?

Well, the number one attraction's called 'Musical Favourites'. Guests enjoy a three-course meal and unlimited free drinks, and watch a fantastic show, starting with musicals set in Paris and then crossing the Atlantic to Las Vegas and finally Copacabana. At the end the <u>cast members come down from the stage</u>, still in their stunning costumes, and <u>you'll have a chance to chat with them</u>. It's hugely popular, so let me know now if you're interested because <u>it's no good leaving it until the last minute</u>. It's on Friday night. Tickets are just 50 euros each, but for an extra 10 euros you can have a table right by the stage.

Q17

Q18

If you'd like to go back in time, there's the *Castle Feast* on Saturday evening. It's held in a twelfth-century castle, and you eat in the great courtyard, with ladies in long gowns serving your food. You're given a whole chicken each, which you eat in the medieval way, <u>using your hands instead of cutlery</u>, and you're entertained by competitions where the horseback riders attempt to knock one another off their horses. Then you can watch the dancers in the ballroom and <u>join in as well if you want</u>. OK, so now if anyone …

Q19

Q20

SECTION 3

STEPHANIE:	Hello, Trevor.
TREVOR:	Hello, Stephanie. You said you wanted to talk about the course I'm taking on literature for children.
STEPHANIE:	That's right. I'm thinking of doing it next year, but I'd like to find out more about it first.
TREVOR:	OK, well, as you probably know, it's a one-year course. It's divided into six modules, and you have to take all of them. One of the most interesting ones, for me, at least, was about the purpose of children's literature.
STEPHANIE:	You mean, whether it should just entertain children or should be educational, as well.
TREVOR:	Right, and whether the teaching should be factual – giving them information about the world – or ethical, teaching them values. What's fascinating is that <u>the writer isn't necessarily conscious of the message they're conveying</u>. For instance, a story might show a child who has a problem as a result of not doing what an adult has told them to do, implying that children should always obey adults.
STEPHANIE:	I see what you mean.
TREVOR:	That module made me realise how important stories are – they can have a significant effect on children as they grow up. Actually, <u>it inspired me to have a go at it myself</u>, just for my own interest. I know I can't compete with the really popular stories, like the Harry Potter books – they're very good, and even young kids like my seven-year-old niece love reading them.
STEPHANIE:	Mm. I'm very interested in illustrations in stories. Is that covered in the course?
TREVOR:	Yes, there's a module on pictures, and how they're sometimes central to the story.

Q21

Q22

STEPHANIE:	That's good. I remember some frightening ones I saw as a child and I can still see them vividly in my mind, years later! Pictures can be so powerful, just as powerful as words. I've always enjoyed drawing, so <u>that's the field I want to go into when I finish the course</u>. I bet that module will be really helpful.	Q23
TREVOR:	I'm sure it will. We also studied comics in that module, but I'm not convinced of their value, not compared with books. One of the great things about words is that you use your imagination, but with a comic you don't have to.	
STEPHANIE:	But children are so used to visual input – on TV, video games, and so on. There are plenty of kids who wouldn't even <u>try</u> to read a book, so I think <u>comics can serve a really useful purpose</u>.	Q24
TREVOR:	You mean, it's better to read a comic than not to read at all? <u>Yes, I suppose you're right</u>. I just think it's sad when children don't read books.	
STEPHANIE:	What about books for girls and books for boys? Does the course go into that?	
TREVOR:	Yes, there's a module on it. For years, lots of stories, in English, at least, assumed that boys went out and did adventurous things and girls stayed at home and played with dolls. I was amazed <u>how many books were targeted at just one sex or the other</u>. Of course this reflects society as it is when the books are written.	Q25
STEPHANIE:	That's true. So it sounds as though you think it's a good course.	
TREVOR:	Definitely.	

TREVOR:	Have you been reading lots of children's stories, to help you decide whether to take the course?	
STEPHANIE:	Yeah. I've gone as far back as the late seventeenth century, though I know there were earlier children's stories.	
TREVOR:	So does that mean you've read Perrault's fairy tales? *Cinderella, The Sleeping Beauty*, and so on.	
STEPHANIE:	Yes. They must be important, <u>because no stories of that type had been written before, these were the first</u>. Then there's *The Swiss Family Robinson*.	Q26
TREVOR:	I haven't read that.	
STEPHANIE:	The English name makes it sound as though Robinson is the family's surname, but a more accurate translation would be *The Swiss Robinsons*, because it's about <u>a Swiss family who are shipwrecked, like Robinson Crusoe in the novel of a century earlier</u>.	Q27
TREVOR:	Well I never knew that!	
STEPHANIE:	Have you read Hoffmann's *The Nutcracker and the Mouse King*?	
TREVOR:	Wasn't that <u>the basis for Tchaikovsky's ballet *The Nutcracker*</u>?	Q28
STEPHANIE:	That's right. It has some quite bizarre elements.	
TREVOR:	I hope you've read Oscar Wilde's *The Happy Prince*. It's probably my favourite children's story of all time.	
STEPHANIE:	Mine too! And it's so surprising, because Wilde is best known for his plays, and most of them are very witty, but *The Happy Prince* is really moving. <u>I struggled with Tolkien's *The Lord of the Rings* – three long books, and I gave up after one</u>.	Q29
TREVOR:	It's extremely popular, though.	
STEPHANIE:	Yeah, but whereas something like *The Happy Prince* just carried me along with it, *The Lord of the Rings* took more effort than I was prepared to give it.	
TREVOR:	I didn't find that – I love it.	
STEPHANIE:	Another one I've read is *War Horse*.	
TREVOR:	Oh yes. It's about the First World War, isn't it? <u>Hardly what you'd expect for a children's story</u>.	Q30
STEPHANIE:	Exactly, but it's been very successful. Have you read any ...	

SECTION 4

In today's class I'm going to talk about marine archaeology, the branch of archaeology focusing on human interaction with the sea, lakes and rivers. It's the study of ships, cargoes, shipping facilities, and other physical remains. I'll give you an example, then go on to show how this type of research is being transformed by the use of the latest technology.

Atlit-Yam was a village on the coast of the eastern Mediterranean, which seems to have been thriving until around 7,000 BC. The residents kept cattle, caught fish and stored grain. They had wells for fresh water, many of their houses were built around a courtyard and were constructed of stone. The village contained an impressive monument: seven half-tonne stones standing in a semicircle around a <u>spring</u>, that might have been used for ceremonial purposes.   *Q31*

Atlit-Yam may have been destroyed swiftly by a tsunami, or climate change may have caused glaciers to melt and sea levels to rise, flooding the village gradually. Whatever the cause, it now lies ten metres below the surface of the Mediterranean, buried under sand at the bottom of the sea. It's been described as the largest and best preserved prehistoric settlement ever found on the seabed.

For marine archaeologists, Atlit-Yam is a treasure trove. Research on the buildings, <u>tools</u> and   *Q32* the human remains has revealed how the bustling village once functioned, and even what diseases some of its residents suffered from. But of course this is only one small village, one window into a lost world. For a fuller picture, researchers need more sunken settlements, but the hard part is finding them.

Underwater research used to require divers to find shipwrecks or artefacts, but in the second half of the twentieth century, various types of underwater vehicles were developed, some controlled from a ship on the surface, and some of them autonomous, which means they don't need to be operated by a person.

Autonomous underwater vehicles, or AUVs, are used in the oil industry, for instance, to create <u>maps</u> of the seabed before rigs and pipelines are installed. To navigate they use sensors,   *Q33* such as compasses and sonar. Until relatively recently they were very expensive, and so <u>heavy</u> that they had to be launched from a large vessel with a winch.   *Q34*

But the latest AUVs are much easier to manoeuvre – they can be launched from the shore or a small ship. And they're much cheaper, which makes them more accessible to research teams. They're also very sophisticated. They can communicate with each other and, for example, work out the most efficient way to survey a site, or to find particular objects on the seabed.

Field tests show the approach can work. For example, in a trial in 2015, three AUVs searched for wrecks at Marzamemi, off the coast of Sicily. The site is the final resting place of an ancient Roman ship, which sank in the sixth century AD while ferrying prefabricated <u>marble</u>   *Q35* elements for the construction of an early church. The AUVs mapped the area in detail, finding other ships carrying columns of the same material.

Creating an internet in the sea for AUVs to communicate is no easy matter. Wifi networks on land use electromagnetic waves, but in water these will only travel a few centimetres. Instead, a more complex mix of technologies is required. For short distances, AUVs can share data using <u>light</u>,   *Q36* while acoustic waves are used to communicate over long distances. But more creative solutions are also being developed, where an AUV working on the seabed offloads data to a second AUV, which then surfaces and beams the data home to the research team using a satellite.

There's also a system that enables AUVs to share information from seabed scans, and other data. So if an AUV surveying the seabed finds an intriguing object, it can share the

coordinates of the object – that is, its position – with a nearby AUV that carries superior
<u>cameras</u>, and arrange for that AUV to make a closer inspection of the object.   *Q37*

Marine archaeologists are excited about the huge potential of these AUVs for their discipline.
One site where they're going to be deployed is the Gulf of Baratti, off the Italian coast. In
1974, a 2,000-year-old Roman vessel was discovered here, in 18 metres of water. When it
sank, it was carrying <u>medical</u> goods, in wooden or tin receptacles. Its cargo gives us insight   *Q38*
into the treatments available all those years ago, including tablets that are thought to have
been dissolved to form a cleansing liquid for the <u>eyes</u>.   *Q39*

Other Roman ships went down nearby, taking their cargoes with them. Some held huge pots
made of terracotta. Some were used for transporting cargoes of olive oil, and others held
<u>wine</u>. In many cases it's only these containers that remain, while the wooden ships have been   *Q40*
buried under silt on the seabed.

Another project that's about to ...

Listening and Reading answer keys

TEST 1

LISTENING

Section 1, Questions 1–10

1 Canadian
2 furniture
3 Park
4 250 (sterling)
5 phone
6 10(th) September
7 museum
8 time
9 blond(e)
10 87954 82361

Section 2, Questions 11–20

11&12 *IN EITHER ORDER*
    A
    C
13&14 *IN EITHER ORDER*
    B
    E
15 B
16 B
17 C
18 A
19 A
20 C

Section 3, Questions 21–30

21 B
22 A
23 C
24 B
25 A
26 B
27 A
28 F
29 G
30 C

Section 4, Questions 31–40

31 industry
32 constant
33 direction
34 floor
35 predictable
36 bay
37 gates
38 fuel
39 jobs
40 migration

If you score ...

0–18	19–27	28–40
you are unlikely to get an acceptable score under examination conditions and we recommend that you spend a lot of time improving your English before you take IELTS.	you may get an acceptable score under examination conditions but we recommend that you think about having more practice or lessons before you take IELTS.	you are likely to get an acceptable score under examination conditions but remember that different institutions will find different scores acceptable.

TEST 1

READING

Reading Passage 1,
Questions 1–13

1   creativity
2   rules
3   cities
4&5   *IN EITHER ORDER*
   traffic
   crime
6   competition
7   evidence
8   life
9   TRUE
10 TRUE
11 NOT GIVEN
12 FALSE
13 TRUE

Reading Passage 2,
Questions 14–26

14 E
15 C
16 F
17 C
18 A
19&20   *IN EITHER ORDER*
   B
   D

21&22   *IN EITHER ORDER*
   D
   E
23 activists
24 consumerism
25 leaflets
26 police

Reading Passage 3,
Questions 27–40

27 E
28 D
29 B
30 D
31 C
32 YES
33 NO
34 NO
35 NOT GIVEN
36 restaurants
37 performance
38 turnover
39 goals
40 characteristics

If you score …

0–17	18–26	27–40
you are unlikely to get an acceptable score under examination conditions and we recommend that you spend a lot of time improving your English before you take IELTS.	you may get an acceptable score under examination conditions but we recommend that you think about having more practice or lessons before you take IELTS.	you are likely to get an acceptable score under examination conditions but remember that different institutions will find different scores acceptable.

TEST 2

LISTENING

Section 1, Questions 1–10

1	219 442 9785
2	10(th) October
3	manager
4	Cawley
5	knee
6	3 weeks
7	tennis
8	running
9	shoulder
10	vitamins

Section 2, Questions 11–20

11	B
12	C
13	C
14	B
15	A
16	H
17	D
18	F
19	A
20	E

Section 3, Questions 21–30

21	B
22	C
23	A
24	A
25	E
26	D
27	A
28	H
29	G
30	C

Section 4, Questions 31–40

31	dances
32	survival
33	clouds
34	festivals
35	comets
36	sky
37	instruments
38	thermometer
39	storms
40	telegraph

If you score...

0–17	18–26	27–40
you are unlikely to get an acceptable score under examination conditions and we recommend that you spend a lot of time improving your English before you take IELTS.	you may get an acceptable score under examination conditions but we recommend that you think about having more practice or lessons before you take IELTS.	you are likely to get an acceptable score under examination conditions but remember that different institutions will find different scores acceptable.

TEST 2

READING

Reading Passage 1,
Questions 1–13

1 FALSE
2 TRUE
3 NOT GIVEN
4 FALSE
5 NOT GIVEN
6 TRUE
7 FALSE
8 TRUE
9 merchant
10 equipment
11 gifts
12 canoe
13 mountains

Reading Passage 2,
Questions 14–26

14 F
15 C
16 E
17 D
18 B
19 design(s)

20 pathogens
21 tuberculosis
22 wards
23 communal
24 public
25 miasmas
26 cholera

Reading Passage 3,
Questions 27–40

27 vi
28 i
29 iii
30 ii
31 ix
32 vii
33 iv
34 viii
35 productive
36 perfectionists
37 dissatisfied
38 TRUE
39 FALSE
40 NOT GIVEN

If you score ...

0–18	19–27	28–40
you are unlikely to get an acceptable score under examination conditions and we recommend that you spend a lot of time improving your English before you take IELTS.	you may get an acceptable score under examination conditions but we recommend that you think about having more practice or lessons before you take IELTS.	you are likely to get an acceptable score under examination conditions but remember that different institutions will find different scores acceptable.

TEST 3

LISTENING

Section 1, Questions 1–10

1	Tesla
2	microphone
3	exhibition
4	wifi
5	45
6	135
7	pool
8	airport
9	sea
10	clubs

Section 2, Questions 11–20

11&12	*IN EITHER ORDER*
	A
	E
13&14	*IN EITHER ORDER*
	B
	E
15	F
16	A
17	E
18	G
19	D
20	C

Section 3, Questions 21–30

21	50
22	regional
23	carnival
24	drummer
25	film
26	parade
27	D
28	B
29	E
30	F

Section 4, Questions 31–40

31	violin
32	energy
33	complex
34	opera
35	disturbing
36	clarinet
37	diversity
38	physics
39	dance
40	Olympics

If you score...

0–17	18–27	28–40
you are unlikely to get an acceptable score under examination conditions and we recommend that you spend a lot of time improving your English before you take IELTS.	you may get an acceptable score under examination conditions but we recommend that you think about having more practice or lessons before you take IELTS.	you are likely to get an acceptable score under examination conditions but remember that different institutions will find different scores acceptable.

TEST 3

READING

Reading Passage 1,
Questions 1–13

1 B
2 A
3 D
4 NOT GIVEN
5 NO
6 YES
7 B
8 C
9 B
10 A
11 A
12 C
13 A

Reading Passage 2,
Questions 14–26

14 C
15 H
16 A
17 F
18 I
19 B
20 E

21&22 IN EITHER ORDER
  B
  C
23 ecology
24 prey
25 habitats
26 antibiotics

Reading Passage 3,
Questions 27–40

27 B
28 G
29 F
30 E
31 C
32 NO
33 YES
34 NOT GIVEN
35 NO
36 YES
37 encouraging
38 desire
39 autonomy
40 targeted

If you score …

0–17	18–26	27–40
you are unlikely to get an acceptable score under examination conditions and we recommend that you spend a lot of time improving your English before you take IELTS.	you may get an acceptable score under examination conditions but we recommend that you think about having more practice or lessons before you take IELTS.	you are likely to get an acceptable score under examination conditions but remember that different institutions will find different scores acceptable.

TEST 4

LISTENING

Section 1, Questions 1–10

1   85
2   roses
3   trees
4   stage
5   speech
6   support
7   cabins
8   C
9   A
10   B

Section 2, Questions 11–20

11   G
12   D
13   A
14   E
15   F
16   B
17&18   *IN EITHER ORDER*
     B
     D
19&20   *IN EITHER ORDER*
     A
     D

Section 3, Questions 21–30

21   A
22   C
23   A
24   B
25   B
26   F
27   E
28   C
29   B
30   G

Section 4, Questions 31–40

31   spring
32   tools
33   maps
34   heavy
35   marble
36   light
37   camera(s)
38   medical
39   eyes
40   wine

If you score...

0–18	19–27	28–40
you are unlikely to get an acceptable score under examination conditions and we recommend that you spend a lot of time improving your English before you take IELTS.	you may get an acceptable score under examination conditions but we recommend that you think about having more practice or lessons before you take IELTS.	you are likely to get an acceptable score under examination conditions but remember that different institutions will find different scores acceptable.

TEST 4

READING

Reading Passage 1, Questions 1–13

1 four / 4
2 young
3 food
4 light
5 aggressively
6 location
7 neurons
8 chemicals
9 FALSE
10 TRUE
11 FALSE
12 NOT GIVEN
13 TRUE

Reading Passage 2, Questions 14–26

14 B
15 E
16 C
17 A
18 TRUE
19 TRUE
20 NOT GIVEN

21 FALSE
22 NOT GIVEN
23&24 *IN EITHER ORDER*
 B
 D
25&26 *IN EITHER ORDER*
 B
 E

Reading Passage 3, Questions 27–40

27 FALSE
28 NOT GIVEN
29 FALSE
30 TRUE
31 FALSE
32 TRUE
33 NOT GIVEN
34 large
35 microplastic
36 populations
37 concentrations
38 predators
39 disasters
40 A

If you score ...

0–17	18–26	27–40
you are unlikely to get an acceptable score under examination conditions and we recommend that you spend a lot of time improving your English before you take IELTS.	you may get an acceptable score under examination conditions but we recommend that you think about having more practice or lessons before you take IELTS.	you are likely to get an acceptable score under examination conditions but remember that different institutions will find different scores acceptable.

Sample answers for Writing tasks

TEST 1, WRITING TASK 1

SAMPLE ANSWER

This is an answer written by a candidate who achieved a **Band 6.5** score.

The diagrams illustrate the average proportions of three types of nutrients in typical meals, which can be unhealthy if consumed too much. The three types include sodium, saturated fats and added sugar. The data is taken from the United States of America.

The first chart shows the average percentages of sodium. Dinner contains the most sodium (43%). Breakfast and snacks include an equal proportion of sodium consumed, with each of them adding up 14% of sodium. Through eating lunch, 29% sodium is consumed. The second chart shows the percentages of saturated fat in meals. By eating dinner, 37% saturated fat is consumed. Lunch contributes to a consumption of 26% saturated fat, followed by snacks with 21% and breakfast with 16%. The last chart illustrates the proportions of added sugar. Snacks contain the highest amount of added sugar (42%). Dinner includes 23% A typical dinner includes 23% added sugar, while lunch contains 19% and breakfast includes 16%.

All in all, the diagrams show that every typical meal consumed in the USA contains a percentage of at least 14% of nutrients that can be unhealthy if eaten too much.

Here is the examiner's comment:

> The candidate has accurately reported the data for each chart and has presented a summary of the information, but could achieve a higher score by making comparisons across the charts, e.g. breakfast contains the lowest amounts of sodium, saturated fats and added sugar. The information is logically organised and there is a clear progression throughout the script. The main points are clearly signalled [*The first chart* | *The second chart* | *All in all*] and there are examples of other cohesive devices [*each of them*]. The range of vocabulary is varied [*data* | *contains* | *an equal proportion of* | *consumed* | *consumption* | *illustrates*]. Minor errors do not cause misunderstanding [*adding up 14% of sodium*]. There is a mix of simple and complex sentence structures, using active, passive and modal verb forms and there is also subordination through the use of participles [*Through eating lunch* | *By eating dinner* | *followed by*]. More variety in grammatical structures would perhaps achieve a higher score.

TEST 1, WRITING TASK 2

SAMPLE ANSWER

This is an answer written by a candidate who achieved a **Band 7.0** score:

Some people believe that it is best to accept a bad situation, such as an unsatisfactory job or shortage of money. Others argue that it is better to try and improve such situations.

Based on my knowledge, some people choose to accept the fate that they have to undergo the bad situation as they believe that good things might come out of it. Their solution is simply to just go with the flow because they think that they will learn something new along the journey. For example, a student received a grade B for his Physics examination. However, he only needs one more mark to get an A. If a student requires to receive a mark percentage of 70% to get an A, this student got a 69% on his paper. As the teacher looked through the questions with the whole class, he notices that the teacher accidentally marked his correct answer to wrong. So, realistically, he should get an A. However, he chooses to leave his grade as a B because he believes that his current grade will be a motivation for him to improve and work harder to get a better grade in the next examination. Hence, this explains why some people chooses to accept the bad situation.

Besides that, it is also mentioned that others argue that is better to try and improve such situations. I believe the reason they act that way is because they feel a bit paranoid that the situation will become worse if they do not do so. For instance, a person had to undergo a shortage of money. Logically, they will feel a little paranoid that at one point, they might have to experience an empty pocket and had to live in the streets. Regarding that matter, they figured out a solution to improvise such situations by getting an extra or part-time job. This solution will help them to gain extra money to pay their daily expenses such as water and electricity bills. This means that their problems are solved and they are now worry-free.

In my honest opinion, I strongly suggest that one can choose to act in both situations according to situations. When facing a problem, think of the best solution to solve it. If the situation requires you to simply ignore it, then just do so. There is a no need in figuring out a way to improve those situations as it will take up your time and cause stress. However, if the situation requires you to take action quickly, by all means do so as you might not know what are the consequences if you ignore the problem.

In a conclusion, the main important thing when facing bad situations is to analyze the problem, then only you can react to them. Not all bad situations needs to be ignored and not all needs to be improved. Think wisely to get the best solution for all of your problems.

Here is the examiner's comment:

> The candidate has addressed all parts of the task and shows a clear position throughout the response. Ideas are presented, extended and supported. The response is logically organised and there is a clear progression throughout,

with a range of cohesive devices [*Based on | For example | However | Hence | Besides that | Regarding that matter | This solution | This means that | In my honest opinion*], with only occasional awkwardness or error [*act in both situations according to situations | In a conclusion*]. Each paragraph contains a clear, central topic. The range of vocabulary includes some less common items [*fate | paranoid*] and shows examples of style and collocation [*go with the flow | figured out a solution | problems are solved | my honest opinion*]. Occasional errors do not prevent the message from coming through. There is a range of grammatical structures and these are usually accurate, although there are a few errors [*some people chooses | might not know what are the consequences | Not all bad situations needs to be ignored*]. The meaning is still clear, however.

TEST 2, WRITING TASK 1

SAMPLE ANSWER

This is an answer written by a candidate who achieved a **Band 6.0** score:

The value of a country's exports may vary in various categories in different years. Usually, the percentage of changes of exports earning will differ by year and category. Here is some information about a country's exports earning based on the year 2015 and 2016.

First, I will start with the country's most money-making export which is petroleum products. By the year 2016, the country gained 3% more in the category than the year 2015. However, for gems and jewellery, the percentage of the export earning decreased by 5.18% by the year 2016.

Next, engineered goods earnings also follow the foot steps of petroleum product earnings by gaining more than 8% on 2016 than 2015. The value increases from more than 50 billions to more than 60 billions in just a year. This statistic also conclude that the engineers in the country have gained more by the year 2016.

Besides that, agricultural products and textiles also earned more with 0.81% and 15.24% respectively. Even though, agricultural products does not gain more than 1%, it stills conclude that the products are still wanted by many people as it earned about more than 30 billions for both years.

While for textures, it is seen that it gains it popularity in the year 2016. This is proved, when the statistic states that the earning was increased by more than 15.24% in the year 2016 based on the year 2015. Textiles products earned about more than 25 billions in 2015 and earned more than 30 billions in the next year.

In conclusion, we can see that this country has overall succeed in the year 2016 than the year 2015. The country managed to gain about more than 22% in the year 2016. Even though gems and jewellery had a decreasing of earnings by 5.18%, it is still the third money-making export product from the country.

Here is the examiner's comment:

> The response covers all the key features and presents an overview in the final paragraph. However, the rating could be improved by providing data in $ billions for earnings for each product (not just engineered goods and textiles). One of the comments is debatable [*This statistic also conclude that the engineers in the country have gained more by the year 2016*]. Organisation follows the order of the bar chart, providing an overall progression, and there is some use of cohesive devices to signal a change of topic. The vocabulary used provides some variety of expression [*differ* | *gained* | *decreased*], even if it is not always appropriate [*money-making* / profitable | *textures* / textiles]. Errors occur [*earning*(s) | *foot step* / footstep | *stills*], but the intended meaning is clear. The candidate uses both simple and complex sentence forms, but better control of both grammar and punctuation might result in a higher rating here.

TEST 2, WRITING TASK 2

MODEL ANSWER

This model has been prepared by an examiner as an example of a very good answer. However, please note that this is just one example out of many possible approaches.

Some people consider that the loss of individual species of plants and animals is the main environmental problem of our time. Attempts to preserve rare or dying species are carried out in zoos or other specialist plant and animal facilities, through breeding programmes, preservation orders and other forms of protection and there was genuine sadness among many when the last surviving white rhino died earlier this year.

Survival of the fittest is nature's way of ruthlessly allowing weaker specimens to die out, although mankind has also contributed to falling animal numbers through hunting and poaching. However, whether saving individual species should be the main focus of environmental protection is debatable. Climate change and excessive use of plastic are just two other major problems that deserve our attention.

The evidence of climate change is there for us all to see: rising sea levels and associated flooding with the loss of homes at low land levels are becoming more frequent. Many countries and island communities are now calling for urgent action to delay, halt or even reverse the process, although if we believe the experts, reversal is impossible. Habitable areas are gradually shrinking, often for some of the poorest groups of people, but there seems to be little obvious action taking place. If the major contributors to climate change will not support the reduction of greenhouse gases, there is little hope for the future.

Naturalists have also begun to expose the serious problems arising from discarded plastic waste. Birds and animals can die gruesome deaths through being trapped or caught up in plastic bags or ropes, while the long process required for these plastics to decay means that they remain a threat for many years to come. Worse, there is now beginning to be evidence of sea creatures ingesting smaller globules of disintegrating plastic, which harms them and all the other creatures in their particular food chain.

The loss of particular species, both flora and fauna, is cause for regret, but I do not agree that they are the most important environmental problems these days. If climate change and damage from plastic continue, there will be less land and less food for everyone, including plants and animals.

TEST 3, WRITING TASK 1

SAMPLE ANSWER

This is an answer written by a candidate who achieved a **Band 6.0** score:

A hydroelectric power station can generate electric power by using the energy of water flowing from high level to low level. It works different functions in day and night.

In the day time, water in the high-level reservoir go through the intake under the dam which is only open in day time. Then the water flow into the power station in which there is a generator. The generator is operated by a reversible turbines that can transfer the water flowing force to the mechanical force which is the power of the generator. The generated electricity then goes to the national grid through the power lines.

On the other hand in the night time, the power station works in a reversed way. It pumps water from the low-level reservoir to high-level reservoir to provide the enough water for day time's work. The water is pumped by the same reversible turbines from low-level reservoir. So the power station actually consumes energy at night. But that is in order to generate more power in the day time.

In a conclusion, a hydroelectric power station can generate power is based on the differce heighth of water level. In day time, it uses the natural water energy. Meanwhile in the night, it transfers the water to create and store the energy for the next day.

Here is the examiner's comment:

> The answer covers the key features of the process and provides an overview of this process in the final paragraph. The detail is not always clear, but the key features are adequately highlighted. Information is arranged coherently and there is a clear overall progression. Cohesive devices are used to signal different stages of the process [*Then* | *On the other hand* | *So* | *In a conclusion* | *Meanwhile*], and there is some use of pronouns for reference [*It* | *which* | *that*]. The range of vocabulary is adequate for the task [*energy* | *operated by* | *transfer* | *mechanical*], in spite of some errors in word form [*a reversed way*] and spelling [*differce heighth*]. There is a mix of simple and complex sentence forms and grammatical control is generally adequate, though there are some errors in the use of articles.

TEST 3, WRITING TASK 2

SAMPLE ANSWER

This is an answer written by a candidate who achieved a **Band 5.5** score:

I agree with this topic. In my opinion I think that music can join anypeople who has different culture together, Music can make a relationship between people all around the world. Although it has different rhytum but when the people who listen to music, their feeling will be better. For the example the woman who will be mom in the future she can use music to join between mom and her baby. I have known about how to make the patients feel better and some cases of the patients in the hospital, the doctors will use music for them. When they patients listen to music (solf music) it makes them feel better. And now we don't use music only human we can use it with animals and plants too.

Music can make us feel better, although we are different ages, nationalities and culture. when we like the same kind of music. We can join and listen together. One more example I have friend and he is the foreigner. He is around 25 years old. He likes to go anywhere with me and he likes to listen Thai song, especially song for life. He tries to practice to sing Thai song and he can do it. Now he can sing many Thai songs.

Including I think music has some power to make human's mind. And it can make good relationship between people who has different ages, cultures and nationalities.

Here is the examiner's comment:

> The response shows a clear position that is relevant to the task, with examples to support the main ideas. There is a clear overall progression, with effective use of cohesive devices [*this* | *them* | *it*] in spite of some errors [*For the example* | *they patients* | *Including* / In conclusion?]. Paragraphing is adequate. Vocabulary is generally adequate, but control over spelling and word choice is weak [*anypeople* | *rhytum* | *solf* / soft? | *anywhere* / everywhere? | *song for life*?], sometimes causing difficulty for the reader. There are attempts at complex sentences, but these usually contain errors [*people who has* | *Although … but when*], and punctuation is sometimes faulty (incorrect capitalisation, misuse of commas and full stops). Better control over spelling, grammar and punctuation might improve the overall score.

TEST 4, WRITING TASK 1

MODEL ANSWER

This model has been prepared by an examiner as an example of a very good answer. However, please note that this is just one example out of many possible approaches.

Grange Park was opened in 1920, a rectangular area with access from Arnold Avenue on the north side and from Eldon Street on the south side. There was a fountain in the centre, with a stage for musicians situated centre left, a glasshouse to the right of the Eldon Street entrance and a pond for water plants in the north east corner opposite. Around the edges of the park there were rose gardens, with seats nearby for people to smell the flowers and listen to music.

The park has altered considerably since then. Now there is one large-ish rose garden, occupying the central area where the fountain stood, and with seats all around it. One of the smaller rose gardens remains on the north side of the park. The bandstand (stage for musicians) has also been replaced, by an amphitheatre for concerts and associated seating. The glasshouse has gone and in its places is a water feature; similarly, where the pond for water plants stood there is now a children's play area with a café nearby. Access to the park is still via the two original entrances, but there is now a third entrance near the water feature from an underground car park.

Despite the apparently significant changes, the park retains the basic elements of flowers, water, seating and music, with the addition of a café and a children's play area.

TEST 4, WRITING TASK 2

SAMPLE ANSWER

This is an answer written by a candidate who achieved a **Band 7.5** score:

Most contemporary economies allow such a model of employment as being self-employed, which appears very tempting for many. However, still the vast majority of people opt for being employed in a company and not to set up their own business. This essay will attempt to look into the key factors as to why people may prefer entrepreneurship and major drawbacks to it.

To start with, in many modern societies, including Russian, entrepreneurship is greatly encouraged with lots of business seminars and workshops advertised. These may range from slightly fraudulent to genuinely educational and supportive, and generally any information on setting up a company is easily accessible for those who are willing. And willing they are, as being a business person, the image itself has a certain feel of luxury, respectability and success. People are being told that they have no limits and can easily become as wealthy as a Steve Jobs is they wish it.

This first reason is linked to the second, which is relevant for Russia and some other counties. Bank loans are accessible too, and they are largely eagerly granted. If a future business person truly knows their business, it poses no threat. Nevertheless, easy access to setting up a company for someone inexperienced or insensible may cause a range of problems.

Apparently, the first issue that may perplex an unskilled entrepreneur is the necessity to be a jack of all trades (if the company is very small). Having taken the responsibilities of an accountant, PR or HR manager at the same time can be a burden and make the person wish they had never done it at all. If they hire other people to perform these tasks, they must pay more tax and provide their employees with decent working conditions. At the same time, business is usually a risky matter and in our competitive reality many of them go bankrupt. And last, but not least – self-employed people are the only people responsible for their own vacations, sick or maternity leaves or any job perks.

So, in a nutshell, being your own master has many downsides, that is why many people decide to play it safe.

Here is the examiner's comment:

> The candidate has produced a well-developed response to the task. Further ideas could be included, e.g. wanting to develop own ideas, wanting to work more flexibly than employment allows for. There is a clear progression throughout the response, with information and ideas organised logically. There is a range of cohesive devices [*To start with* | *These* | *The first ... the second* | *Apparently* | *last but not least*] and each paragraph has a clear central topic. There is a wide range of vocabulary, including less common items and showing evidence of style and collocation [*contemporary* | *tempting* | *vast majority* | *opt for* | *entrepreneurship* | *fraudulent* |

image | *luxury* | *perplex* | *jack of all trades*], with only rare examples of inaccuracy [*insensible*]. There is a variety of complex structures, used flexibly and accurately. Grammar and punctuation are well controlled and there are frequent error-free sentences. A few errors persist [*still the vast majority of people opt for* (word order) | (the) *major drawbacks*] but the message is still clear.

Sample answer sheets

BRITISH COUNCIL

idp

Cambridge Assessment English

IELTS Listening Answer Sheet

Candidate Name

Candidate No.

Centre No.

Test Date   Day   Month   Year

Listening Listening Listening Listening Listening Listening Listening

Marker use only

1		21	
2		22	
3		23	
4		24	
5		25	
6		26	
7		27	
8		28	
9		29	
10		30	
11		31	
12		32	
13		33	
14		34	
15		35	
16		36	
17		37	
18		38	
19		39	
20		40	

Marker 2 Signature:

Marker 1 Signature:

Listening Total:

20656

Sample answer sheets

BRITISH COUNCIL **idp** **Cambridge Assessment English**

IELTS Writing Answer Sheet - TASK 1

Candidate Name

Candidate No.   Centre No.

Test Module   ☐ Academic   ☐ General Training   Test Date Day   Month   Year

If you need more space to write your answer, use an additional sheet and write in the space provided to indicate how many sheets you are using: Sheet   of

Writing   Task 1   Writing   Task 1   Writing   Task 1   Writing   Task 1

Do not write below this line

Do not write in this area. Please continue your answer on the other side of this sheet.

23505

Sample answer sheets

Acknowledgements

The authors and publishers acknowledge the following sources of copyright material and are grateful for the permissions granted. While every effort has been made, it has not always been possible to identify the sources of all the material used, or to trace all copyright holders. If any omissions are brought to our notice, we will be happy to include the appropriate acknowledgements on reprinting and in the next update to the digital edition, as applicable.

Reading – Test 1: *The Guardian* for the text adapted from 'Story of cities #30: how this Amsterdam inventor gave bike-sharing to the world' by Renate van der Zee, *The Guardian*, 26.04.2016. Reproduced with permission; *The Guardian* for the text adapted from 'Why zoos are good' by Dr Dave Hone, *The Guardian*, 19.08.2014. Reproduced with permission; Adapted text from 'Play's the thing' by Louise Walsh, *Horizons*, Issue 27, June 2015. Copyright © 2015 Cambridge University Press. Reproduced with kind permission; Adapted text from 'Motivational Factors And The Hospitality Industry: A Case Study Examining The Effects Of Changes In The Working Environment' by Thomas Marshall. Copyright © Clute Institute. Reproduced with kind permission of Thomas Marshall & Clute Institute; **Test 2:** Text adapted from 'Say yes to mess – why companies should embrace disorder' by Dinuka Herath. Copyright © 2017; **Test 3:** Text adapted from 'Saving bugs in the name of drugs' by Ross Piper. Copyright © 2017 Syon Geographical Ltd. Reproduced with permission; Courtesy of Minnesota Children's Museum and Dr Rachel E. White. Reproduced with permission; **Test 4:** Copyright © 2016 *The Atlantic Media Co.*, as first published in TheAtlantic.Com. All rights reserved. Distributed by Tribune Content Agency; Copyright © 2016 Smithsonian Institution. Reproduced with permission from Smithsonian Enterprises. All rights reserved. Reproduction in any medium is strictly prohibited without permission from Smithsonian Institution. Reproduced with permission. **Listening – Test 1:** *The Guardian* for the text adapted from 'New technologies bring marine archaeology treasures to light' by Ian Sample, *The Guardian*, 29.12.2016. Reproduced with permission.